Cambridge Elen

Elements in Race, Ethnicity, and Politics
edited by
Megan Ming Francis
University of Washington

WOMEN VOTERS

Race, Gender, and Dynamism in American Elections

Jane Junn
University of Southern California

Natalie Masuoka
University of California, Los Angeles

CAMBRIDGE
UNIVERSITY PRESS

CAMBRIDGE
UNIVERSITY PRESS

Shaftesbury Road, Cambridge CB2 8EA, United Kingdom

One Liberty Plaza, 20th Floor, New York, NY 10006, USA

477 Williamstown Road, Port Melbourne, VIC 3207, Australia

314–321, 3rd Floor, Plot 3, Splendor Forum, Jasola District Centre,
New Delhi – 110025, India

103 Penang Road, #05–06/07, Visioncrest Commercial, Singapore 238467

Cambridge University Press is part of Cambridge University Press & Assessment,
a department of the University of Cambridge.

We share the University's mission to contribute to society through the pursuit of
education, learning and research at the highest international levels of excellence.

www.cambridge.org
Information on this title: www.cambridge.org/9781009494625

DOI: 10.1017/9781009326889

First published 2024

A catalogue record for this publication is available from the British Library.

ISBN 978-1-009-49462-5 Hardback
ISBN 978-1-009-32687-2 Paperback
ISSN 2633-0423 (online)
ISSN 2633-0415 (print)

Additional resources for this publication at www.cambridge.org/Junn-Masuoka

Women Voters

Race, Gender, and Dynamism in American Elections

Elements in Race, Ethnicity, and Politics

DOI: 10.1017/9781009326889
First published online: June 2024

Jane Junn
University of Southern California

Natalie Masuoka
University of California, Los Angeles

Author for correspondence: Natalie Masuoka, nmasuoka@ucla.edu

Abstract: *Women Voters* documents and explains three important phenomena implicating gender, race, and immigration. The Element contributes to a better understanding of partisan candidate choice in US presidential elections. First, women are diverse and politically heterogenous, where white women are more likely to vote Republican and women of color are majority Democratic voters. Second, due to the unequal privileges and constraints associated with race, white women have greater agency to sort by partisan preference, whereas women of color have more limited choice in their partisan support. Finally, the authors emphasize compositional change in the electorate as an important explanation of electoral outcomes.

Keywords: gender, voting, partisanship, intersectionality

ISBNs: 9781009494625 (HB), 9781009326872 (PB), 9781009326889 (OC)
ISSNs: 2633-0423 (online), 2633-0415 (print)

Contents

Online appendices are available at:
www.cambridge.org/Junn-Masuoka

Introduction

This Element has been a long time in the making, initiated to some degree by frustration with the narrative around gender and race in the 2016 election, both in the popular press and in scholarly work. The errors in description and inference were so obvious but at the same time so difficult to dislodge, which along with the disruptions of the pandemic, lengthened the amount of time it took to complete the analysis and writing. In retrospect, the longer time horizon was beneficial because more things happened and could be absorbed and analyzed. These years saw the development of movements including #MeToo, which encouraged publicly identifying perpetrators of sexual assault, abuse, and harassment; "Time's Up" which shed further light on misogynistic practices in the workplace; and "Black Lives Matter" which further ignited racial justice movements. Anti-Asian violence, an ever-present reality amplified by the coronavirus pandemic, in conjunction with persistent restrictive and punitive immigration policies targeting Latinx people, continued to keep negative sentiment against people of color in the United States at a steady boil. And then the US Supreme Court issued the *Dobbs* decision overturning the precedent of the right to abortion, followed shortly thereafter by its decision on affirmative action. The politics of race and gender thus remain at the top of the political agenda for voters and politicians.

The title of the Element belies the complexity of sex and gender, and in terms of nomenclature, the terms "woman/women" and "female" are used interchangeably, despite the fact that gender as a category of self-identification exists on a continuum, and the fact that sex is most often used to signify a biological trait in binary terms. While it is regrettable that all expressions of gender identity and a more accurate continuum of sex cannot be represented in the data, we were constrained by the persistent measurement of gender and sex in binary terms. In future data collections and analyses, we will do better.

1 Women Voters

The past two decades in US politics have been anything but boring. Out of six elections between 2000 and 2020, two propelled the loser of the popular vote into the White House based on a win in the Electoral College, the outcome of one of these elections was decided only after a 5–4 ruling by the US Supreme Court. During this time, the Democratic Party nominated the first-ever Black candidate at the top of a national party ticket as well as the first-ever woman candidate, in addition to a first-ever woman of color as the vice-presidential nominee in 2020. While all of these Democratic Party candidates would succeed in winning the majority of Americans' votes, Hillary Clinton's loss in the Electoral College to Donald Trump in 2016 gave pause to the lie of gender equality in US politics, dashing the hopes of supporters that her widely anticipated victory would finally shatter the glass ceiling for women in politics.

Celebrations marking the first woman President of the United States remain on ice, and as gendered as the 2016 contest was, and despite the fact that both of the candidates and their running mates were white, the politics of race in the United States helped pave the way for Trump's unlikely successes. Distinguishing itself as a protector of traditional values and conservatism, the Republican Party since the Civil Rights era has remained consistent in opposition to policies promoting equality on the basis of both race and sex, including voting rights and abortion. In step with maintaining existing racial and gender hierarchy, among the most provocative statements by then-candidate Trump – about "Mexican rapists" and his penchant to grab women "by the pussy" – were candid assertions of the place of white men at the apex of power. Embraced by majorities of white voters and male voters in 2016 and 2020, Trump's electoral coalition was characterized by both race and gender. His successes in winning the Republican Party's nomination were powered by groups that preceded his run for the White House – including the "Tea Party" that mobilized fear and resentment in reaction to President Barack Obama – and later by groups that developed alongside his presidency such as the "Proud Boys," carrying their potent message of masculinity and white nationalism.

Nevertheless, the expectation was widespread that Clinton's historic candidacy would elicit strong electoral support among American women. The persistence of a gender gap of women voters favoring Democratic Party candidates (compared to men) added fuel to the fire of anticipation of the United States electing its first woman president. News and prediction outlets including the Upshot in *The New York Times* published Election Day updates showing high probabilities for a Clinton victory. The Upshot gave strong odds to Clinton (85%) over Trump, with an analogy to men's sports: "Mrs. Clinton's chance of losing is about the same as the probability that an N.F.L. kicker misses a 37-yard field goal."[1] Even Fox News was pessimistic about a Trump victory the day before the election, publishing results of a recent poll showing Clinton with

---

[1] For the Upshot prediction see: www.nytimes.com/interactive/2016/upshot/presidential-polls-fore cast.html.

a 4-point lead.[2] Despite losing the popular vote, Trump would defy the odds and defeat Clinton in the Electoral College. Exhortations by trailblazing women in politics such as former US Secretary of State Madeline Albright, who admonished women to support women, went unheeded by the majority of white women voters.[3]

Absorbing the outcome of the 2016 US presidential election, journalists, pollsters, political commentators, and scholars attempted to explain how and why it happened. Clinton's loss was set in sharp relief to the expectation that women would support a woman candidate because elected officials and women voters alike are seen as politically liberal and associated more closely with the Democratic Party (Huddy and Terkildsen 1993; McDermott 1997; Koch 2000; Palmer and Simon 2008; Thomsen 2015). Among the most perplexing questions was how Trump won despite his words and actions and with the presence of a substantial gender gap in party preference for Democrats among woman voters. Compared to men, and in the aggregate, women voters favored the Democratic Party candidate by a margin of 54% to 41%, but because traditional definitions of the gender gap are calculated as the *difference between men and women in supporting the winning candidate*, the race reflected an 11-point "gender gap" (men for Trump at 53% versus 42% among women).[4] Further, given widespread condemnation of the Republican candidate in the "Access Hollywood" video released just weeks before the election, why didn't voters – especially women voters – reject him and choose her instead? Clinton was, after all, a descriptive representative for woman voters and specifically white women. In the end, it was women of color and Black women voters in particular who were her stalwart supporters, whereas white woman voters chose Trump by a 9-point margin.

Among the most comprehensive studies of Clinton's 2016 loss is a sober post-election analysis from the Barbara Lee Family Foundation's "Presidential Gender Watch" undertaken by the Center for American Women and Politics (CAWP) at Rutgers University. The report provides a thorough walk through the gendered context of elections, focusing on standards of candidacy, raising questions about the extent to which women voters were effectively mobilized to turn out, and problematizing the concept of "the women's vote" (CAWP 2017). Despite covering a range of factors, one key element in the dynamics of the election is not discussed until the final pages of the report, and the

---

[2] www.foxnews.com/politics/fox-news-poll-clinton-moves-to-4-point-edge-over-trump.
[3] [www.washingtonpost.com/video/politics/madeleine-albright-stumps-for-clinton/2016/02/06/f42095dc-cd1e-11e5-b9ab-26591104bb19_video.html].
[4] CAWP 2017: https://cawp.rutgers.edu/sites/default/files/resources/ggpresvote.pdf.

significance of race and ethnicity are acknowledged in a section bearing the question, "Did Women Abandon Clinton?" About women of color, the report dutifully notes: "These women voters have been the key to Democratic candidates' success and that remained true in 2016" (CAWP 2017, p. 27). But to introduce the fact that white women voters supported Trump by a majority, the report relied on comedian Samantha Bee to break the news (CAWP 2017, p. 27).

Gender and Race as "Both/And" in Partisan Vote Choice

As is revealed in the forthcoming pages, race is a key factor in explaining how and why gender is important in American elections.[5] Instead of beginning with the prior that either gender or race is dominant, the story of women voters is a dynamic tale of race and gender working together to affect the electoral fortunes of candidates for US president. By contrast, and in the immediate wake of the 2016 election, some experts prioritized the impact of gender – and in Clinton's case, the deficit of being a woman (Reston 2016) – by arguing that gender is more polarizing to voters than race. Accounts such as these are incomplete at best, and there can be no more denying that women voters in US presidential elections vary substantially, and that race is a key element of the divergence. Acknowledging this does not mean that gender is unimportant and that only race matters. Instead, gender and race exist in a "both/and" rather than an "either/or" relationship for partisan vote choice in elections. Consider the counterfactual of another Obama running for and winning the American presidency in 2008 and 2012; that it had to be him and not her is a clear example of how race and gender work together rather than separately as "either/or." Former First Lady Michelle Obama cannot be either a woman or an African American because she is simultaneously "both/and" (Gay and Tate 1998).

Simple as this insight may appear to be, the impulse to fold all within gender at the expense of recognizing cross-cutting cleavages with competing categories of marginalization such as race is both strong and undeniable. Being "either/or" and on the sharp end of the stick remains a potent rallying cry to mobilization. Certainly, women have been subjugated, disenfranchised, and at best ignored in US politics, but the form and degree to which this is the case intersects with race and ethnicity. For example, while the 100-year anniversary of the ratification of the Nineteenth Amendment was celebrated, it was only

---

[5] By "gender" we compare only two categories of women and men voters. We recognize that gender identity is not limited to only these two and we hope future research can explore a more complex gender identity that recognizes gender beyond this dichotomy. See our discussion in the Acknowledgements section in the Online Appendix.

white women who universally gained suffrage in 1920. In contrast, women of color would wait another half-century for federal voting rights legislation to secure their enfranchisement across the nation.

Put more concretely, while Hillary Clinton's grandmother would have gained access to the ballot box with the ratification of the Nineteenth Amendment, Michelle Obama's did not. And, of course, Trump's male ancestors would not have needed constitutional amendment for enfranchisement. The reality of this historical context represents the contours of agency and constraint within the broader structure of US democratic institutions and practices defined and structured by white heteropatriarchy (Strolovitch, Wong, and Proctor 2017). The history of the right to vote for some and its flip side of systematic disenfranchisement for others in the United States create an intersectional dynamic of restriction based on gender and race. Similarly, voter preferences developed within the institutional context of the ideological positions of US political parties reflect the divergence between the two major parties on issues of civil rights and women's rights.

Thus the context within which voters align with political parties, make decisions about which candidates to support, and are mobilized to turn out are structured by hierarchies of advantage and marginalization based in both gender and race. While political discourse rarely implicates explicit justifications for the enfranchisement of men and whites alone, the legacy of the status of white men in particular as both the "modal voter" and the typical candidate for US president persists. Neither Trump nor Biden had to be referred to with race and gender modifiers in 2020 because both existed within the "default category" of presidential candidates. In contrast, and precisely because Hillary Clinton was an anomaly as the first woman to run on a major party ticket for president, she was often referred to as a female candidate, modified by a category of political marginalization in a similar way that Barack Obama was described as an African American presidential candidate. Conversely, going unnamed by race and gender signifies the privilege of being typical.

While women candidates for president may be anomalous, by contrast, women voters are far from unusual, and it is women, rather than men, who are the modal voters in US presidential elections. Data supporting this fact have been visible in the public record for decades, and the first important correction to conventional wisdom about gender and elections is the recognition that women voters are the largest gendered group in the electorate. A second update to the dynamics of gender and elections is simultaneously obvious and yet ignored. Far from a monolith, the category of women voters is one that represents a heterogeneous group in terms of political interests and partisan support, both of which intersect with race and ethnicity (Huddy, Cassese, and Lizotte 2008). While analysts routinely cite the variation, the structural context and consequences of racial diversity among women voters is nevertheless frequently elided by misleading stereotypes about women voters as Democratic Party supporters.

While the large crowds of white women wearing pussy hats and marching in protests following Trump's inauguration illustrated their support of Hillary Clinton in 2016, these women are in fact in the minority among white women voters overall. Instead, more white women voted for Trump, in 2016 and again in 2020, a pattern of support for Republican Party candidates set decades ago. At the same time, white women also make up the largest piece of the diverse coalition of Democratic Party supporters in those two elections. Instead of being a contradiction, these facts illustrate the "both/and" nature of gender and race that coexists in the dynamics of US presidential elections. Thus, and from a broader perspective of analyzing American voting behavior, that women are both heterogeneous and the modal voter demonstrates with clarity that gender and race should be front and center in any analysis of US elections.

Obvious as this pattern is, political analysts and scholars of contemporary US politics have identified the fault lines around race and gender, but tend to do so separately in either/or fashion. In contrast, we argue that race and gender should be analyzed together simultaneously with an intersectional approach that considers the variation in agency of choice among voters based on both race and gender. Being white or a person of color and being a man or woman are more than individual-level traits to be "controlled for" in analysis. Instead, these identity markers also signify positionality within the twin and overlapping structures of racial hierarchy and patriarchy as locations with more or less constraint on political behavior and choices at the individual level.

Women Voters Are the Modal Voter

It bears reminding that women have been included in the American electorate for only the past 100 years, and that the right to vote was at first extended universally only to white women (Keyssar 2009). Prior to this, for the first century and a half of the history of the United States, women were nearly invisible in politics. The introduction of women voters into the American polity began in earnest after the ratification of the

Nineteenth Amendment and resulted in a steady rise in women's voting participation throughout the twentieth century (Corder and Wobrecht 2016; Wolbrecht and Corder 2020). Four decades into their formal enfranchisement, American women voters overtook men in turnout. What is clear from the data in Figure 1 detailing the gender composition of the electorate over the last sixty years is that there have been more women voters than men since the time political scientists began collecting systematic survey data from individuals. Nevertheless, and at that time, the picture in the mind's eye of the American voter was that of a white man; a representative agent that could be aggregated to draw conclusions about political behavior in the macro polity.

This normative position is evident in Campbell, Converse, Miller, and Stokes's classic work, *The American Voter*, published in 1960, where they concluded this about women voters in the United States: "Women who tend to 'leave politics to the menfolks' even though they are willing to go to the polls register here as having a more impoverished level of political concept formation" (p. 492). Campbell et al. mollified concern that politically unsophisticated

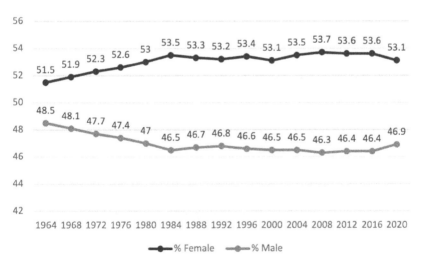

Figure 1 Gender composition of the American electorate, 1964–2020

Source: The data used to create this figure was sourced from the Center for American Women and Politics website: https://cawp.rutgers.edu/facts which presents analysis of the US Census Bureau Current Population Survey P20 reports

women voters would cause instability in the electorate, claiming that wives would follow their husbands.

> The wife who votes but otherwise pays little attention to politics tends to leave not only the sifting of information up to her husband but abides by his ultimate decision about the direction of the vote as well. The information that she brings to bear on "her" choice is indeed fragmentary, because it is second hand. Since the partisan decision is anchored not in these fragments but in the fuller political understanding of the husband, it may have greater stability over a period of time than we would otherwise suspect. (p. 492)

Among the conclusions to the ten-page section titled "Sex" in *The American Voter* is the assessment that there is no discernible and gender-related pattern in voting behavior. "In the current era, there is no reason to believe that women *as women* are differentially attracted to one of the political parties" (emphasis original, p. 493).

The passage of time has not diminished the influence of early scholarship to set assumptions about the relationship between gender and power in the electorate, and therefore the way partisan candidate choice is studied. While the predispositions of these initial observations to frame how to analyze and interpret voting behavior are difficult to dislodge, it is clear that both the conclusions and the analytical practices supporting them are in dire need of correction.

Women Voters Are Diverse

Contrary to this early research from the 1950s and 1960s, patterns of voting behavior from subsequent decades identified a partisan gender gap in candidate and party preference, voting turnout, and policy positions (Sapiro and Conover 1997; Norrander 2008). Scholarship from the 1980s and onward showed women held different political views from men, and the finding that women favored Democrats became part of a new conventional wisdom on the gender gap (Kaufmann and Petrocik 1999; Kaufmann 2006; Blinder and Rolfe 2018; Deckman and Cassese 2021).

Journalists and political analysts along with scholars continue to toe this line, expecting women to support Democratic Party candidates for US president in particular. While women overall show majority support for Democrats, this aggregated result is a function of the heavily lopsided Democratic preferences of African Americans, Latinas, Asian Americans, and other women of color voters who now make up more than a quarter of women voters in the United States.

Table 1 Number and proportion of women
voters by Race, 1980–2020

	White women (millions)	Women of color (millions)
1980	44.0	6.1
1984	47.7	7.8
1988	47.7	7.9
1992	52.9	8.9
1996	48.1	9.4
2000	47.1	12.0
2004	52.5	13.9
2008	53.1	16.3
2012	51.8	18.5
2016	53.1	19.7
2020	65.0	23.5

Source: The data used to create this figure was
sourced from the Center for American Women
and Politics website: https://cawp.rutgers.edu/
facts which presents analysis of the US Census
Bureau Current Population Survey P20 reports

Table 1 details the changes in the composition of the women voting population in
the United States between 1980 and 2020, based on an analysis of US Census
Current Population Survey (CAWP 2022). Several patterns in the data in Table 1 are
noteworthy. During the Reagan years, white women made up 86–88% of women
voters while women of color (including African American and Latina voters)
represented 12–14% of the women electorate.[6] In the elections that followed, the
number of minority voters expands rapidly due to the implementation of voting
rights legislation and the growth in Latin American and Asian immigration. Women
of color voters now make up more than a quarter of the women electorate.
Consequently, women voters became much more diverse, and the proportion of
women of color voters exceeds a quarter of all women voters, having quadrupled in
numbers from 6.1 million in 1980 to 23.5 million in 2020.

The significance of this dynamism in the population of American voters
overall and women voters in particular is the effect it has on the composition
of supporters of the nominees for US President for each of the two major
political parties in the United States. While we detail the distribution by race

---

[6] Prior to 2000, "women of color" includes Black and Latina women. After 2000, Asian Americans
   are included.

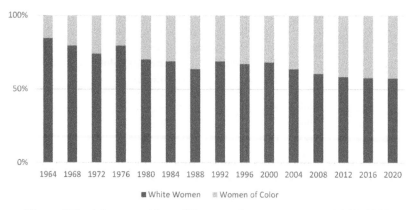

Figure 2 Racial composition of Democratic women voters, 1964–2020
Source: ANES

and gender in the next section, Figure 2 provides a window into the magnitude of importance women of color play in the Democratic Party coalition.

Over time women of color have grown to make up an increasing share of the Democratic coalition, approaching nearly half of all that party's women supporters in 2016 and 2020. This persists despite the fact that white women make up 73% of women voters and just over half of Democratic Party supporters. As we will demonstrate in a forthcoming section, the data in Figure 2 presage the results that show patterns of support for Democrats, and indeed the development of the gender gap in partisan candidate choice that is driven by the steadily increasing presence of women of color voters in the electorate who bring with them strong and consistent support of that party's nominees.

Women Voters Are Increasingly Racially Diverse While Republicans Remain White

The rapid increase in racial diversity among women voters is the result of the reduction of race-based exclusion from voting due to federal civil rights, voting rights, and immigration legislation of the 1960s. The consolidation of African Americans into the Democratic Party took another two decades to complete and occurred at just the time when the electoral consequences of the 1965 Immigration and Nationality Act began to be felt (Tate 1993; Segura and Bowler 2011). Despite the enactment of amendments to the US Constitution guaranteeing that the right to vote not be denied on the basis of sex and race, the inclusion of voters of color – whether in the United States for generations or recently arrived – and their full enfranchisement remains a work in progress. Long-standing disenfranchisement on the basis of US territorial residence continues to keep out millions of potential voters (Sparrow 2006). In addition, contemporary efforts to disqualify voters have multiplied following the US Supreme Court's decision in *Shelby County* (2013), particularly in southern states.

Variation by race and ethnicity in candidate choice would not be relevant for analyzing election outcomes unless there was companion variation in partisan candidate choice by race. Figure 3 presents data from the American National Election Study visualized as stacked bar charts of the gender-race composition of voters who cast their ballots for the Democratic versus Republican Party candidate for US president in 1968 and 2020. In the earlier election, non-white voters were mostly African Americans, and women and men voters of color made up 21% of the Democratic Party's base of support in 1968. As the composition of the population of the nation and the electorate changed, that proportion was more than 40% in 2020. This pattern stands in stark contrast to the data for support of Republican Party candidates among voters of color. For both Republican candidates in those elections – Nixon and Trump – their voter base is heavily and disproportionately composed of white voters, whereas non-white voters tally 2% in 1968 and 11% in 2020.

Data on voter demographics are usually not presented in this way, and instead it is more common for analysts to report statistics such as the following: 55–58% of white voters supported Trump in 2020. Useful as these data are, they do not translate to saying that Republican supporters during that election were composed of that proportion of white voters. Instead, the correct answer is

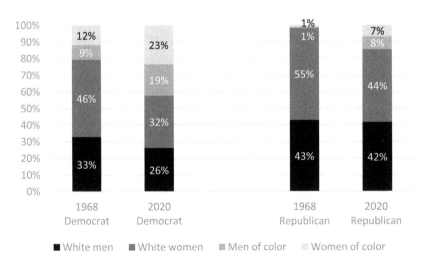

Figure 3 Gender-race composition of Democratic and Republican voters, 1968 and 2020

Source: ANES

that 89% of Trump's voters are white. Similarly, aggregating all Republican Party voters together reveals that the biggest group inside of his coalition of supporters is white women (45%) followed closely by white men (42%). The same pattern is evident for Nixon in 1968, but by a greater margin where white women represented 55% of his supporters compared to 43% for white men. In contrast, the Democratic Party's coalition is a diverse group, with white women leading the way in 1968 for Hubert Humphrey (46%), and voters of color for Joe Biden (43%) in 2020.

The full complement of American National Election Study (ANES) data between 1948 and 2020 puts a finer point on the conclusion that the gender-race composition of Democratic Party supporters has mirrored the diversity of the voting population over time, while the Republican Party has remained heavily composed of white voters. Figure 4 displays the composition of voters who cast their ballots for Democratic Party nominees. As the electorate itself has changed from more than 90% white in the pre–Voting Rights Act era, to around three-quarters white in 2020, Democratic candidates count 43% of their support from voters of color. Nevertheless, the single largest gender-race group of Democratic supporters in 2016 was white women, who made up 32% of Clinton's coalition and 29% of Biden's voters in 2020. While a smaller proportion, white men made up the second largest race-gendered group at 27% for Biden, with women of color following closely behind as the third largest group of Democratic Party supporters.

In contrast, the composition of Republican Party supporters shows a starkly different profile, and the data are displayed in Figure 5. Republican voters have been composed 90% and more of white Americans. Despite the substantial diversification of the US population overall to more than one-third non-white

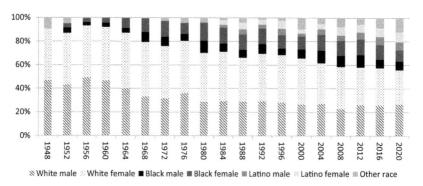

Figure 4 Gender-race composition of Democratic Party voters, 1948–2020
Source: ANES

Racial and Gender Makeup of Republican Voters

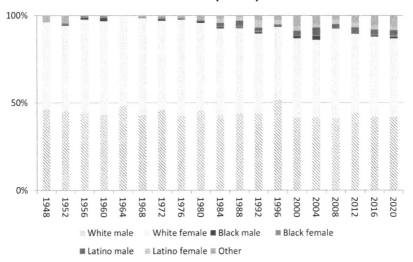

Figure 5 Gender-race composition of Republican Party voters, 1948–2020
Source: ANES

(and roughly a quarter of voters), Republican Party supporters remain heavily dominated by white Americans. A final observation is that the largest group of voters in the Republican coalition in all but one presidential election across the time series (1996) is white women. While white women are more Democratic when compared to white men, they nevertheless still compose the largest portion of the Republican electorate.

These data showing the gender, racial, and ethnic composition of voters who supported Democratic Party candidates versus Republican Party nominees for US president over the last half century and more reveal a stark difference. The coalition of American voters who back Democrats is racially diverse, while those who support Republicans are relatively stable and white. This distinction is a fitting divergence for Democratic Party nominees who have run as the party of change versus Republican Party candidates that conversely have prioritized conserving tradition. Taken together with the data presented at the beginning of this section on the modal voter status of women voters and with their increasing racial diversity, this analysis of compositional change in the US electorate highlights the political power of women voters in choosing the president of the United States.

Taking the lead from these empirical realities, conclusions about women voters should no longer be made in comparison to the default category of men and their party and candidate preferences. Instead, the variation within women voters can be better observed and the patterns that lie within can be marshalled to better explain election dynamics and outcomes. Continuing to ignore the variation in partisan candidate choice among women voters has the consequence of inaccurately stereotyping women as Democratic Party supporters, because while there are plenty of white women voters who support Democrats, there are more who support Republican nominees.

The Story of Women Voters: Roadmap

In the sections to come, a set of important corrections for how we should understand the relationship between gender, race, and electoral outcomes at the individual level are revealed. Grounding this analysis in Section 2 is a conceptual articulation of the context of this heterogeneous behavior that is based in the unequal privileges and constraints associated with race and gender. This intersectional approach begins with the theoretical proposition that Americans are constrained in unequal and systematic ways by their position in the combined structures of patriarchy and the US racial hierarchy (Collins 2008; Hancock 2015; Crenshaw 2017). Both gender and race at the individual level matter and must therefore be analyzed together, following the logic of the salience of social groups and structural inequality (Young 1990).

Section 3 examines the partisan candidate preferences of women of color voters, demonstrating their stalwart support of Democratic Party nominees for US president. Data from the Collaborative Multiracial Post-Election Survey (CMPS) detail the variation between the larger groups of women of color who support Democrats versus the much smaller proportion of African American, Latina, and Asian American women who vote for Republican Party candidates for president. We uncover variation across racial and ethnic minority groups, with Black women voters the strongest and most consistent supporters of Democrats, while recent data collections from 2016 and 2020 evinced strong support among Latinas and Asian American women voters for Hillary Clinton and Joseph Biden.

Switching the focus to white women, Section 4 delves deeper into the diverse partisan politics of white women voters. Using ANES data for analysis, we show that there is substantial partisan diversity among white women and clear variation in the factors that lead white women voters to support Republican Party nominees for president. The analysis in this section reveals the partisan candidate choices of white women since 1988 and highlights their Republican-leaning preferences. The analysis illuminates when factors such as regional location, religion, education, income, and marital status have been significant predictors of white women's preference for Republicans. Wide diversity of partisanship preference, social context, and political attitudes among white women, combined with broader agency to choose sides, results in this group of voters spanning the distance between feminists, career moms, suburban warriors, and handmaidens to patriarchy.

The fifth section reviews the evidence on the gender gap in partisan vote choice in presidential elections based on the conventional wisdom that women voters are Democratic voters. We show that the gender gap in voting in the United States is the result the steady increase of women of color into the electorate who bring their strong and consistent support of Democratic candidates into the voting booth, thereby canceling out majority Republican support among white women. The results provide a comprehensive view of the gender gap within racial groups, as well as a demonstration of the dynamics of the gender gap as a consequence of compositional change in the US electorate over time.

In the concluding section, we reiterate that both race and gender matter in American elections and argue that ignoring one or the other produces faulty predictions and incomplete conclusions. At the same time, while accounting for gender and race together is more complicated than the standard and more conventional analyses political commentators have become accustomed to, an intersectional approach accounting for multiple marginalization, structural and interpersonal, is "a mess worth making" (Smooth 2006). Dynamism in the American electorate both in partisanship and in compositional change that is the result of immigration requires analysts to update their methodological strategies for analysis to better understand how and why US presidential elections are won and lost, and the vital role American women voters play in these contests.

2 Analyzing Both/And: Race, Gender, and Party in Candidate Choice

There are many moving parts in the story of women voters and their role in choosing the President of the United States. As such, no single analytical approach can capture all angles. But a methodology that perceives change, recognizes connections, and acknowledges structural inequalities is most likely to yield a fulsome explanation of past and present as well as better serve in making predictions for the future. Charting a new way forward, this section articulates a conceptual argument for a dynamic and intersectional approach to analyzing candidate choice in US presidential elections, where both gender and race play an important combined role. Distinct from earlier and still-dominant approaches, our methodology for analysis begins by acknowledging the legacy of structural inequalities in enfranchisement and theorizing their continuing significance for American voters. We describe the crucial role political parties play in creating distinct policy positions – with the Republican Party remaining consistent in its anti-egalitarian stance – that produce the conditions under which this party is not a viable choice for Americans who are marginalized on account of being both a woman and a person of color. As such, not all individuals feel the same degree of agency in choosing between candidates of the two major political parties. Together the interconnection between gender and race and the relationship with political parties come together in a dynamic intersectional approach to analyzing partisan candidate choice among women voters in US presidential elections.

The Right to Vote: The Contemporary Legacies of Systemic Disenfranchisement

The legacy of disenfranchisement and the positions of the major political parties on either enhancing or limiting voting rights must be acknowledged and accounted for when analyzing candidate choice among voters in the contemporary context. Significant barriers to inclusion have been based in race, gender, youthful age, class, and citizenship status. The path to voting for women and people of color was both long and arduous in comparison to the exception of the speedy and relatively uncontroversial ratification of the Twenty-Sixth Amendment in 1971, which enfranchised a population of previously excluded voters (ages 18–20) who are not defined in marginalization by either race or gender.

At the founding of the United States it was unnecessary to make arguments defending the extension of the right to vote only to propertied white men, not least of which because they were the ones with standing under the law. Class, in the form of property ownership posed an early hurdle but was eliminated for white males by the mid-nineteenth century. Chattel slavery and the dehumanization of Blacks along with the exclusion of the native inhabitants of the territory were written into and protected by the US Constitution. Protections for white voters continued with passage of the Naturalization Act of 1790 which limited immigrant naturalization to only whites, and being a US citizen remains a necessary condition for casting a ballot in federal elections (Hayduk 2006).

Women won the right to vote first among the systematically excluded but not without fierce opposition. Justifications and rhetoric against woman suffrage were based on the inferior quality of women's minds as well as their natural unsuitability to the violent and unseemly world of politics (Keyssar 2009; Goodie 2012). The argument that women were paragons of moral virtue was simultaneously used by suffragists, doing double duty in claims that the presence of women voters would help to purify politics while juxtaposing the virtues of women against the presumed scourge of Black men. It is precisely the iconic suffragists – Susan B. Anthony and Elizabeth Cady Stanton – who not only privileged the enfranchisement of white women over African Americans, but also actively weaponized their white womanhood to demonize Blacks as unfit for inclusion (Barkley Brown 1997; Terborg-Penn 1998). While coalitions between abolitionists and suffragists were present, the right to vote for white women was in the end won in closer alliance with white supremacists, a broad and deep constituency at the time (Dudden 2011). Among the most potent legacies of the Nineteenth Amendment is the reification of white women in superiority to Black people and other people of color, rendering the latter unworthy of inclusion as voters in the American polity. The right to vote for women secured by the Nineteenth Amendment was thus not universal, but instead a privilege granted to white women.

African Americans and people of color would wait another half-century for the right to vote across the United States. The practice of Jim Crow and the active participation of white women in supporting racial segregation both during slavery and through the Civil Rights era and into the present help to explain why Blacks, Latinos, and Asian Americans were denied the franchise despite the Fifteenth Amendment, which was ratified a century prior to the 1965 Voting Rights Act (Lewis 2006; McRae 2018; Gilmore 2019). Political conservatism and anti-Black racial animus among supporters of the modern Republican Party – no longer the party of Abraham Lincoln – fuel renewed efforts at voter disqualification, and the bitter aftertaste of battles over inclusion in the American polity persists (Schlozman and Rosenfeld 2024).

This toxic amalgamation thwarting egalitarian voting practices in the United States is not simply an accident of history. Rather, the combination of domination on the basis of both gender and race is a case in point of the pairing of the twin impulses of patriarchy and racial supremacy, two ideologies deeply embedded in the history of the United States (see, e.g., Parker and Barreto 2013; Schmidt 2021). Together the elitist impulse for domination by race and gender intersect to create a rapid current of racial hierarchy and patriarchy in the United States that became institutionalized, and as a result is difficult to swim against. In this structural system, men and whites are at the top, Blacks and Native Americans at the bottom for most of the history of the nation, and other groups in between beneath whites (Kim 1999; Masuoka and Junn 2013). Women are not treated equally to men, with women of color distinguished from white women in placement below both men and whites.

How political parties developed over time and into the modern era to either nurture or oppose voting rights for all Americans, and the extent to which ordinary voters would react to the divergence, are the next part of the story of the context of unequal agency and constrained choice by gender and race in the American electorate.

The Parties Diverge: Civil Rights, Women's Rights and the Republican Embrace of Hierarchy

Political parties in the United States have both been altered by and been important actors in the transformation of politics around voting enfranchisement (Abrajano and Hajnal 2015). While the degree of variation between the Republican Party and the Democratic Party in terms of formal platform policies and ideological positions has waxed and waned over time, the two major US political parties since the U.S. Civil Rights era now present distinctive choices for American voters. Eric Schickler's analysis of racial realignment following the Great Depression through 1965 details the stark divide voters and party leaders pressed forward, molding the modern Democratic Party to become relatively more progressive on both civil rights and gender equity, in contrast to the Republican Party's embrace of "racial conservatism" and adherence to traditional gender roles rooted in "social conservatism" (Carmines and Stimson 1989; Schickler 2016).

"Racial conservatism" is a euphemism sometimes used by political scientists to describe Republican Party opposition to voting rights in addition to their early support of racial segregation and accompanying opposition to civil rights. Partisan realignment in the south among white voters took shape in the mid-twentieth century starting with their abandonment of the Democratic Party to support racial segregationist candidates for president, including Strom Thurmond (who ran for the Dixiecrat Party in 1948), Harry F. Byrd (unpledged electors in 1960), and George Wallace (who ran for the American Independent Party in 1968). These contests saw white voters in southern states award their Electoral College votes to candidates who supported the continuation of racial segregation and the disenfranchisement of African American citizens. Eventually, and with Nixon's "southern strategy" in action, white southerners coalesced behind the modern Republican Party, and it was only fifteen years after the passage of the VRA that Ronald Reagan kicked off his 1980 presidential campaign with his "states' rights" speech at the Neshoba County Fairgrounds near Philadelphia, Mississippi.

Republican Party politicians in contemporary politics continue to diminish voting rights, with among the most consequential moves the federal lawsuit brought by Shelby County, Alabama, challenging the constitutionality of crucial provisions of the Voting Rights Act (*Shelby County v. Holder* 2013). Since then, states and localities across the nation, and not just in the American South, passed new legislation regulating voting, making it more difficult to register, to qualify to vote, to vote by mail, and to submit one's ballot (Grose and Bell 2023). Justifying the policies with allegations of voter fraud, Republican state legislatures and politicians alike took a page from past rhetoric on eliminating what they deemed as unqualified and undesirable voters from participating. Efforts at legislative gerrymandering continue this pattern of behavior.

Regarding gender hierarchy, the embrace of "social conservatism" within the Republican Party is most often used to describe opposition to policies on equal pay for women, abortion rights, and LGBT rights, among other issues that challenge traditional gender roles. The record provides ample evidence of Republican Party positions at odds with the policies aimed at attenuating structural inequalities based in race and gender (Milbank 2022; Murib 2023). Opposition to reproductive rights for women, affirmative action for underrepresented minorities, support of restrictive immigration policies, and the embrace of punitive crime policy are among the clearest contemporary issues on which Republican and Democratic Party candidates for office differ (Lowndes 2008). The *Dobbs* (2022) decision by the US Supreme Court overturning the precedent set in *Roe* (1973) that was made possible by the appointment of conservative jurists by a Republican president is the latest example of the divide separating the parties and their candidates on gender equity.

On the flip side and following the southern racial realignment, the modern Democratic Party has supported civil rights and voting rights legislation and policy, and also been at the more supportive of equal rights and gender equity for American women and people of all genders. The imperative to confront and reduce structural inequalities based on race and gender meant that a broader coalition of voters across race, including progressive whites as well as voters of color, could be forged, and for this reason, the composition of supporters of Democratic Party candidates for US president has become racially diverse. As detailed in the previous section, this diversity among Democratic voters exists in stark contrast to the composition of supporters of Republican Party presidential candidates, the latter of whom remain almost 90% white. More than any other indicator, the patterns of support among American voters by race reflects the divergence in these policy positions by the two major political parties.

Yet the fact that white women are stronger supporters of Republican Party candidates than Democratic Party nominees, even when considering the relatively anti-egalitarian policies of the former, demonstrates just how important position in and protection of the racial hierarchy remains in the contemporary context for some white women voters. Republican and conservative white women respond to patriarchy's constraint by embracing it in a trade for racial superiority, and the data and a growing literature on conservative women document the tradeoffs contemporary Republican white women voters make between race and gender (Schreiber 2008; Junn 2017; Och and Shames 2018).

These are the "deep roots" of the intersectional politics of anti-Blackness and white race supremacy that are intimately intertwined with the subjugation of African Americans and Black women in particular, with the active participation of white women (Blee 2002). The construction of "white womanhood" is forged not only by explicitly racist propaganda but has long been nurtured by traditional gender roles and the "social conservatism" represented in contemporary Republican Party platform policies. The role of white women in particular as bearers of children is an important part of the ideology of the protection racket, which requires an exchange for being put on a pedestal and for taking up residence in a gilded cage (de Beauvoir 2011; Sjoberg and Peet 2011; Manne 2017). That some American women choose the velvet glove despite the knowledge that iron fist of patriarchy lies underneath makes sense within the logic of the protection racket (Jackman 1996; Frasure-Yokley 2018).

In contrast, and while the effects of patriarchal structures, institutions, and values influence people of all races and genders, women of color do not have the same agency to choose occupancy in the gilded cage. They are not welcome precisely because of their intersectional location based in gender and race, reflecting the words of Sojourner Truth: "Nobody ever helps me into carriages, or over mud-puddles, or gives me any best place! And ain't I a woman?"

As we will show in the sections to come, the support of Republican Party candidates for president that is dominated by white voters is distinct from patterns of support analyzed separately by race and gender. White women are more evenly split between the two parties, though there is a consistent majority of white women voters supporting Republican Party candidates over time. In contrast, women of color heavily and consistently back Democrats. This pattern in the data – in the face of stronger support of gender egalitarian policies by the Democratic Party – indicates that race and gender are not easily separable. Instead, and as we argue next, intersectional location in the overlapping hierarchies of race and gender acts together to constrain the agency of choice.

An Alternative Explanation of Candidate Choice: Intersectionality and Agency of Choice

Conventional approaches to analyzing voting behavior have for the most part assumed that individuals have equal agency when choosing between candidates running for office. In contrast, we argue that intersectional positionality within the overlapping structures of patriarchy and racial hierarchy constrains unequally, and therefore, analyzing partisan candidate vote choice in US presidential elections requires a distinctive intersectional approach to analysis.

When analyzing large-N survey data of American voters, an empirical intersectional approach is distinct from traditional strategies of including all respondents and specifying "dummy variables" for categories of interest and interaction terms where systematic variation is hypothesized to exist. Instead, an intersectional analysis of empirical data on partisan vote choice should begin by disaggregating the population of voters into separate categories of race and gender, after which statistical models can be estimated with the data. This analytical strategy allows for the observation of distinct patterns within the context of the overlapping structures of racial hierarchy and patriarchy that unequally constrain American voters.

Among women voters, white women make the choice between anti-egalitarian positions on gender and race but can choose superiority in the latter. Alternatively, and despite the fact that they have the same set of candidates on their ballots for US president, women of color have more limited agency in deciding who to support because choosing the party that embraces "racial conservatism" and the traditional gender roles of "social conservatism" means agreeing to second place or lower in both hierarchies defining gender and race. Agency is a loaded term precisely because it covers so much ground, and to be clear, we are not taking the position that women of color have less capacity to act in politics. Black women are among the most active participants in the US political system, taking part in elections and campaigns in myriad ways, working in their communities, contacting officials, and voting for candidates (Simien 2006; Farris and Holman 2014). Rather, agency in the context of choosing between the candidates for US president is constrained for women of color – and African American women in particular – because one of the alternatives presents an existential threat to many of these voters (Brown 2014).

The heavily white voter composition of supporters of Republican Party candidates and its consistency over time provides the first clue that the two parties provide a rational choice based in ideology for white voters only. However, issues implicating "racial conservatism" and "social conservatism" are only part of the policy platform of Republican Party candidates for president, and white voters can choose between the two major parties if their affinities on fiscal and economic policy or foreign policy are more consistent with Republican candidates even if they disagree on inegalitarian policies based in gender and race. They can because they are less immediately affected in a negative way by Republican Party policies of racial and social conservatism. White women voters – still majority supporters of Republican candidates for president – are nevertheless less supportive than their white male counterparts because socially conservative policies on gender equity affect them more negatively than for men. Among white voters, therefore, gender is more constraining for women than it is for men, and the recent dismantling of the precedent on reproductive rights is one example.

In contrast, while minority voters are still free to choose Republican Party candidates over Democrats, they do so with far lower frequency because of the Republican Party's positions on policies supporting the maintenance of unequal positionality on the basis of race. Williams theorized this "constraint of race" for African Americans more broadly in politics as a legacy of white privilege (Williams 2003). Among minority voters, women of color are the most constrained, due to both their race and their gendered status as women. Overall, minority voters could exercise their choice to vote and to support, for example, Republican Donald Trump in 2016 and 2020, but relatively few did so. This underscores the fact that voters of color evaluate the policies and candidates of the Republican Party as providing a less hospitable political location for African Americans, Latinos, and Asian Americans (Tanenhaus 2013). At the same time, we see variation across racial minority groups in their partisan vote choice. Minority voters exercise agency related to their racial position on the hierarchy, with African American voters in particular "captured" by the Democratic Party (Tate 1993; Dawson 1994; Frymer 1999; Philpot 2017; White and Laird 2020).

Thus, it is incorrect to identify either race or only gender alone as influencing variation in partisan preferences and voting behavior among Americans. To the extent that one political party signals a philosophy and policies supporting white racial supremacy and patriarchal dominance of men over women, voters can choose to align or not align with this party. The act of voting for candidates of a party and indeed the decision to turn out to vote are rational responses to signals political parties send to voters. At the same time, and while white women have greater agency than women of color to sort based on their positions on other issues – choosing liberal progressive candidates of the Democratic Party or conservative candidates nominated by the Republican Party – they nevertheless remain constrained by gender and traditional roles assigned to women.

Discussion

Taking account of the legacy of systemic disenfranchisement on the basis of gender and race, and the role of political parties, provides a wider window through which to theorize the conditions under which voters make decisions about which candidate to support in US presidential elections. We advanced the argument that voters do not have equal agency in choice, and that analysts cannot look only to race or only to gender differences to discern the dynamics of candidate choice and voting in US presidential elections.

The next two sections enact this empirical intersectional analytical strategy, beginning with a focus on women of color voters and analyzing separately Black, Latina, and Asian American women in their candidate preferences for US president. We move next to consider the contours and antecedents to the diverse partisan politics of white women voters. This approach to the analysis illustrates the utility of an intersectional analytical approach to revealing how and why diverse women voters are the most influential voters in US presidential elections.

3 Stalwarts of the Modern Democratic Party: Women of Color Voters

Our empirical analysis of the partisan candidate choices of women voters in US presidential elections begins with a detailed examination of the political behavior of women of color, encompassing Black, Latina, and Asian American women voters.[7] A rapidly growing group within the American electorate, women of color are themselves a diverse group, varying by geographic location, nativity, and language, among other things, as well as different experiences with barriers to enfranchisement. Nevertheless, what women of color in the US political system share in common is their intersectional position within patriarchy and racial hierarchy, where their political agency is structured by marginalized status as both women and minorities. Women of color have come a long way in politics, but the dynamics of intersectionality that continue to make it necessary to modify with "both/and" signify how much further we have to go.

Among the most incisive articulations of intersectionality was written by the Combahee River Collective in 1977 (see also Collins 2008; Crenshaw 2017). The National Black Feminist Organization came together to describe how their exclusion from both feminist movements (where the women were white) and civil rights organizations (where the activists were men) was emblematic of multiple and interlocking spheres of subjugation and political marginalization based in race, gender, sexuality, and class. Honoring the American abolitionist Harriet Tubman, the Combahee River Collective's name commemorated a successful slave emancipation mission. Nearly a half-century later, their statement speaks for all women of color:[8] "We also often find it difficult to separate race from class from sex oppression because in our lives they are most

---

[7] Unfortunately most data today do not include sufficient samples of Native American, Middle Eastern and North African, or Native Hawaiian/Pacific Islander women.

[8] See also: Davis 1981; Moraga and Anzaldua 2021; Anzaldua 2022.

often experienced simultaneously. We know that there is such a thing as racial-sexual oppression which is neither solely racial nor solely sexual, e.g., the history of rape of Black women by white men as a weapon of political repression" (CRC 1977, p. 4).

The experiences as women of color contribute to a collective understanding of politics aimed at fighting both racial and gender inequality, and are manifest in politics by the overwhelming support among this group of voters for candidates of the Democratic Party and its positions on policies aimed at enhancing equality. The racial polarization apparent in the modern two-party system means that as racial minorities, women of color prefer the party that has taken a stance supporting both racial and gender equity. In this section, we detail empirical analyses showing overwhelming Democratic support from women of color voters while recognizing their constrained agency to support candidates representing anti-egalitarian platforms on issues related to race and gender.

Thus while women of color form the backbone of voter support for Democrats, their political activism and leadership for the party are often taken for granted, called upon and noticed only when needed.[9] Reflecting on the observation that all the feminists are white, and all the civil rights activists are men (Hull and Bell-Scott 1993), the visibility of women of color in politics has been obscured by the attention to white women as progressives and feminists. As is clear from decades of data on partisan candidate preference, the evident irony lies in the fact that this focus on white women in politics persists in the presence of their majority support of Republicans. In contrast, and despite being a core and therefore a key constituency of Democratic Party coalitions, much less is known about the political behavior of women of color. Few sources are readily available to describe their characteristics, or about the factors that encourage partisan voting preferences. To address this void, our analysis puts women of color first and unfolds the core argument that because of their intersectional location as well as their position of relative constraint in agency of choice, women of color are much more likely to embrace social justice–oriented positions and candidates.

At the same time, a section focusing on women of color voters should not intentionally or unintentionally reduce the complexity of this diverse group to a stereotype of the prototypical woman of color voter. Instead, the analysis is mindful of variation within the larger group as well as within the group classifications of Black, Latina, and Asian American. Although women of color are strong supporters of Democratic Party nominees for president, they are not politically uniform, and instead vary in important ways. Consistent with

---

[9] For example: www.nytimes.com/2020/10/13/opinion/megan-thee-stallion-black-women.html.

a growing scholarship that disaggregates by both race and gender (Pardo 1998; Harris, Sinclair-Chapman, and McKenzie 2005; García-Bedolla and Scola 2006; Simien 2006; Farris and Holman 2014; Stout, Kretschmer, and Ruppanner 2017; Wong 2018; Matos, Greene, and Sanbonmatsu 2021; Phillips 2021; Lien and Filler 2022; Carey and Lizotte 2023), adopting an intersectional approach to analysis provides the opportunity to reveal variation within groups. The analysis that follows thus disaggregates African American, Asian American, and Latina women voters and their partisan candidate choice for president in 2016 and 2020. The results illuminate the diverse, yet constrained, politics of women of color voters in US presidential elections.

Both/And: Organizing for Progressive Change But Constrained to Support Democrats

The distinctive politics of women of color and their political activism has received relatively scant attention despite the fact that Black, Latina, and Asian American women have been central to organized efforts seeking to challenge racial and gendered oppression. Anti-slavery movements and securing the right to vote were among the first issues of political action among African American women, beginning with Sojourner Truth and progressing through the US Civil Rights movement with icons such as Rosa Parks and Fannie Lou Hamer (Blain 2021; Larson 2021). Black women's activism has thus been a constant in US politics and is well documented in the historical record (Bay et al. 2015; Gilmore 2019). Their activity has continued, unabated, despite substantial barriers, to rise above those hurdles. Some Black women leaders target institutional change by entering elected office such as Shirley Chisholm, who was one of the first women to run for US president in 1972, while others focus their efforts outside of electoral politics by leading political movements for social justice, including Black Lives Matter co-founders Patrice Cullors, Alicia Garza, and Opal Tometi.

Similarly, Latina and Asian American women have advocated for progressive social change on a diversity of issues including labor organizing, environmental justice, immigration, prison reform, and voting rights. These women have been on the forefront of progressive politics in the United States for decades, though their names are less well known and many of their stories are yet to be told. A more focused examination of these activists demonstrates a commitment to social change but at the same time diversity across the content and character of their activism. Among the icons of the American labor movement is Dolores Huerta, a major figure who co-founded the National Farmworkers Association with Cesar Chavez. Citizen activist groups such as the Mothers of East Los Angeles were organizing for environmental justice in the 1980s, holding state government entities and private corporations accountable for polluting local communities (Pardo 1998; Gilmore 2007; Jaramillo 2010; Milkman and Terriquez 2012; Montoya and Seminario 2020).

Asian American women's activism ranges from an embrace of radical politics to a more incrementalist approach. This is exemplified by their efforts within social justice movements. Civil rights activist Yuri Kochiyama embraced the radical politics of the Black Panther Party, while Pasty Takemoto Mink, the first Asian American woman elected to the US House of Representatives, sponsored and helped pass Title IX into law (Fujino 2002; Wu 2022). Activists such as Helen Zia organized pan-ethnic movements by bringing together different Asian national origin groups to see a shared racialized experience (Zia 2001). Researchers Michi Nishiura Weglyn and Aiko Herzig-Yoshinaga brought to bear evidence used for redress for Japanese American interment (Weglyn 1966). Grace Lee Boggs and, more recently, Ai-Jen Poo are on the front lines for workers' and tenants' rights (Choy 2005; Bao 2006; Fujiwara and Roshanravan 2018), while other Asian American women such as Cecelia Chung advocate for LGBTQ rights.

Given that women of color embrace progressive political agendas, their support for Democratic candidates in the voting booth since the last partisan realignment makes intuitive sense. But their support of Democratic candidates should also be understood in terms of the constraints they experience in the US two-party system rather than simply characterizing them as Democratic Party loyalists. The overwhelming support among women of color for Democrats belies their diverse political opinions and visions for change in challenges to the status quo. Their political goals often did not, or could not, align with mainstream political parties, and their alignment as a core constituency within the Democratic Party was neither easy nor without controversy.

Support in kind from political parties has often not matched the disproportionate votes from women of color. For example, the Democratic Party chose to seat an all-white delegation from Mississippi at its 1964 national convention. A challenge was led by Fannie Lou Hamer, who described in vivid detail the murderous violence against Blacks attempting to register to vote. Hamer's words describing the arrests, incarceration, and violent beating she endured are preserved and ends with the statement:

> All of this is on account we want to register, to become first-class citizens, and if the freedom Democratic Party is not seated now, I question America, is this America, the land of the free and the home of the brave where we have to sleep with our telephones off of the hooks because our lives be threatened daily because we want to live as decent human beings, in America?

Hamer and fellow delegates from the Mississippi Freedom Democratic Party implored national party leaders to seat them at the convention, but they were denied, and media coverage of her powerful speech was interrupted when President Lyndon Johnson gave a press conference at exactly the same time (Larson 2021).

Thus, disproportionate votes for Democratic over Republican candidates among women of color do not necessarily imply that they feel strong positive attachment or loyalty to the Democratic Party, or that the party is responsive or representative of their political interests. Instead, the divergence between the two major American political parties today provides little choice for women of color voters because candidates representing the Republican Party today have aligned with positions inconsistent with enhancing egalitarian outcomes in politics that benefit women of color. These voters face constraint at the ballot box because the only plausible candidates to represent them are Democrats, even though these politicians may not fully represent the political interests of women of color.

Women of Color Democratic *Voters* Reflect the Diverse Women of Color *Electorate*

Our argument builds on the observation that "captured voters" have more limited options when one of the parties in a two-party system embraces anti-egalitarian policies on race. Under these circumstances, there is only one viable option for African American voters to support, other than to abstain from voting (Frymer 1999). The situation for women of color voters is similar, if not more exaggerated, given the contemporary Republican Party's positions on issues of gender equity. Thus, the solidly Democratic Party preferences of women of color in part reflect the lack of options they have in the voting booth, and as a result, Latina, Black, and Asian American women voters experience less agency of choice in voting relative to white women voters.

Voting studies have long described partisan vote choice as the result of individuals' assessment of which party best represents their interests (Hajnal and Lee 2013). In the context of polarization, the two major US political parties have staked out clear and opposing issue positions that allow for sorting of groups into each of the parties (Levendusky 2009). But this sorting occurs primarily among white voters because political parties have been the most responsive to their political interests and policy positions. For women voters, the expectation that sorting will occur along demographic characteristics – urban, educated, and unmarried for Democrats and evangelical, working class, and married for Republicans – applies to explanations of white women voters, and less so for women of color. For example, white evangelicals are among the strongest loyalists in the Republican Party (Layman 2001). But these same indicators do not have the same sorting effect for women of color. Instead, scholars have shown that religious conservativism does not translate into strong Republican preference for Asian Americans or Latinos (Wong 2018). Similarly, while narratives emphasizing crime motivate white suburban women to embrace Republican Party candidates (Mendelberg 2001; Riismandel 2020), these messages do not sort Black and Latino voters to Republican support (White 2007; Ramirez 2015). Instead, women of color vote heavily Democratic despite their diversity in terms of those individual-level characteristics deemed consequential for partisan choice.

One useful metric of agency in partisan voting is the degree to which women voters can sort based on their individual level traits. Among women of color, we should not expect there to be as many individual-level factors that predict support of Democrats versus Republicans because of their intersectional position and status as captured voters in a two-party system. In contrast, white women have greater agency in choice because they can vote for the partisan candidate that best represents their identities or interests, and a number of individual-level factors systematically predict vote choice for Republicans versus Democrats. That said, the constraint of intersectionality is not uniform among women of color. Building on our previous work (see Masuoka and Junn 2013) we argue that race constrains life chances for Asian American and Latina women differently from that of Black women. In terms of the US racial order, Blacks are at the bottom of the hierarchy, with Latinos the next lowest in rank, followed by Asian Americans. This order is important to recognizing the structural location from which women of color exercise agency in choosing candidates for US president.

Among women of color voters, Black women have the least agency in partisan candidate choice, given that these voters experience the heaviest social and economic constraints attributed to their race and gender. This translates into near-unanimous support for Democratic Party candidates (Tate 1993; Dawson 1994; Simien 2006). Because nearly all Black women vote for Democrats, we hypothesize that the empirical analysis will reveal that there are few, if any, individual-level predictors of their partisan vote choice. Among other women of color, we anticipate that proportionally more Asian American women voters believe that they hold agency in partisan choice. Although the historical and present racialized treatment of Asian Americans leads them to demonstrate greater support for Democrats over Republicans, Asian Americans do not always see themselves as a marginalized racial minority group. Studies on Asian American racial attitudes show that a good share of Asian Americans do not see their race to impact their life chances to the same degree as voters from other racial minority groups (Leung, Kim and Masuoka, forthcoming). Furthermore, Asian American women's greater integration with whites as evidenced by their high intermarriage with white men (Qian and Lichter 2007), residential patterns in white neighborhoods (Iceland and Wilkes 2006), and employment in professional fields (Dhingra 2007) also leads to varied political preferences within the group. Given this, we expect to find that while Asian American women vote in the majority for Democrats, there will be more individual-level variation explaining the partisan vote choice among Asian American women compared to Black women voters.

We expect the pattern for Latina voters to fall between that of Black and of Asian American women voters. Like African American women, many Latinas today experience severe marginalization as a group, and so politically are constrained to support Democratic candidates. Latinas are a more heavily immigrant group and conduct the invisible labor needed to support a growing economy which create conditions of vulnerability to abuse and unequal treatment (Hardy Fanta 1993; Hondagneu-Sotelo 1994). These shared conditions lead Latinas to support Democratic candidates, in addition to anti-immigration Republican Party positions that have been increasingly racialized as anti-Latino (Chavez 2013; Ramirez 2013; Abrajano and Hajnal 2015). At the same time, Latinas are a more politically heterogeneous group compared to Black women because Latinas as a group are diverse in terms of national origin and immigration status (Beltran 2010). US relations with Latin American countries also means that certain Latino national origin groups have been treated differently, which leads to varied experiences of marginalization by national origin group (Portes and Bach 1985). For example, research shows that some national origin groups such as Cubans are strong Republican supporters while others support the Democratic Party (Fraga et al. 2011). Taken together, we expect that because immigration is a core source of variation among Latinas, we will likely find that Latina vote choice systematically varies along immigration-related characteristics.

Data and Methods

In these next sections, we primarily analyze data collected by the Collaborative Multiracial Post-election Survey (CMPS) which fields nationally representative post-election surveys with sizeable oversamples of Black, Latino, and Asian American respondents (Frasure et al. 2016; Frasure et al. 2020; see Online Appendix Table A3.1). As a study targeting racial minority populations, the CMPS is conducted in multiple languages and aims to collect a full cross-section of minority populations in the United States. CMPS is one of the few political surveys available that offer the opportunity to compare across racial minority groups. Moreover, given the large sample size of each racial minority group, CMPS enables the opportunity to compare Democratic and Republican minority voters. In contrast, national surveys like ANES collect relatively small samples of minority respondents, thereby offering less statistical leverage to explore the internal variation of any one group of minority voters.[10] Given that we aim to analyze three women of color groups across multiple elections, there are many comparisons to be drawn, and therefore to accomplish a more straightforward analysis, we analyze data from the two most recent presidential elections of 2016 and 2020.

Our objective in this section is to understand and identify the types of women of color voters who support Democratic candidates and observe if there are clear differences compared to women of color voters who support Republican candidates. For each election year, we calculate the demographic and other individual-level traits of Democratic and Republican women of color voters.[11] We consider those factors established in the literature as informing partisan preferences for women including socioeconomic status, marital and family status, religiosity, regional location, and sexuality (Campbell et al. 1960; Hajnal and Lee 2011). Given our focus on Latina and Asian American women voters, we also consider factors related to immigration such as nativity and national origin.

Black Women Voters

For Black women voters, the first question is, who is the average Black woman Democratic voter and who is the average Black woman Republican voter? In other words, what kinds of factors influence Black women to be Democratic voters compared to Republican voters? In the CMPS data, nearly all (93%) Black women voted for the Democratic candidate in both 2016 and 2020 (see Figure 6). The overwhelming share of Black women who vote Democratic is consistent across election cycles demonstrating that their support is solidly Democratic.

Since nearly all African American women vote Democratic, the first important pattern to note is that Black women Democratic voters generally represent the

---

[10] See Online Appendix A, Tables A3.3, A3.4, which offers calculations using ANES, and Online Appendix A, Table A3.6 from the National Asian American Survey and by Pew. A comparison across surveys confirms the general patterns found using CMPS data to hold across ANES, NAAS, and Pew. However, we caution that a reliable comparison across surveys is difficult to make since survey instruments vary across surveys.

[11] Online Appendix B summarizes the survey items.

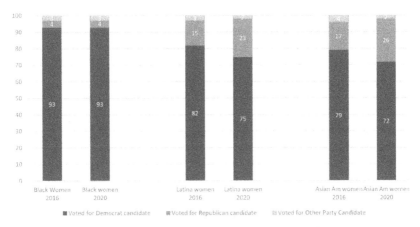

Figure 6 Vote choice among Black, Latina, and Asian American Women Voters in 2016 and 2020 CMPS

Sources: 2016 and 2020 CMPS

population of Black women voters overall. Therefore, many demographic characteristics that define Black women Democratic voters are those factors that predict being a voter. Black women Democratic voters on average are more educated and older than the general population of Black women, which is consistent with our understanding that those with more resources are more likely to participate in politics (Verba, Schlozman, and Brady 1995) (see Table 2). But on other characteristics not necessarily related to voting participation, we find that Black women Democratic voters are representative of the Black women population. For example, Black women Democratic voters are largely from the South, which is reflective of the residential patterns of the African American population as a whole (see Online Appendix Table A.3.2 for full results).

Of course, there is a small minority of Black women Republican voters in every election. Is there a systematic difference that differentiates Black women Republican voters from the Black women Democratic majority? To answer this, we first examined the general demographic makeup of Democratic and Republican Black women voters in 2016 and 2020 using CMPS. In Table 3, the percentages report the demographic characteristics of Black women Democratic voters and of Black Republican voters for each election. We then calculated a difference of proportion to understand if there are statistically significant differences in the characteristics between Black women Democratic and Republican voters. If the differences are statistically significant, the numbers are highlighted in bold in the table.

Table 2 Comparing age and socioeconomic status of Black
women Democratic voters and Black women in the general
population in the 2020 election

	2020 Presidential election	
	Black women voters	**Total population of Black women**
Avg age	50	45
% College educated	30	23
Avg family income	$60 k–$64.9	$45 k–$49.9 K

Source: 2020 ANES

Table 3 Demographics of Democratic and Republican Black women voters in
2016 and 2020 CMPS

	2016		2020	
	Clinton voters	**Trump voters**	**Biden Voters**	**Trump voters**
Share of Black women voters	96	4	96	4
Age				
% Under 30	11	12	7	10
% Over 64	19	25	26	18
Socioeconomic status				
% HS degree or less	34	42	28	28
% College degree	**25**	**14**	33	31
% HH Income < $50k	64	62	52	51
% HH Income >100K	10	9	15	20
% Employed	38	28	38	33
Family Structure				
% Married	29	34	33	37
% Single	41	53	32	28
% Children in HH	76	79	27	34

Table 3 (cont.)

	2016		2020	
	Clinton voters	Trump voters	Biden Voters	Trump voters
U.S. Region				
% Lives in South	56	50	57	55
Religion				
% Evangelical	**37**	**55**	**10**	**27**
% High Church Attend	24	28	40	44
Identity				
% LGBQ	6	3	**5**	**2**

Sources: 2016 and 2020 CMPS

Notes: Percentages are rounded to the nearest whole number. Data were weighted to align with the population estimates calculated from 2019 ACS. Bolded cells reflect statistically significant differences between Democratic and Republican voters at p<0.05.

Comparing the breakdown of Black women Democratic and Republican voters, we find that while it might appear at first glance that there are raw differences across the characteristics of age, socioeconomic status, and family formation, most of these differences are not statistically significant. To further confirm if these differences are significant, we specified a logistic regression to predict support for the Democratic candidate among Black women voters (see Online Appendix Table A3.3 for full model results). In 2016, we find that only two individual-level factors reach statistical significance for predicting vote choice: marital status, and evangelical religious affiliation. In 2016, we find that holding all other factors constant, Black women who were single and unmarried relative to Black women with all other martial statuses were more likely to support the Republican candidate. Those who identified as evangelical were more likely to support the Republican candidate. In 2020, we also find two factors to systematically predict vote choice: age and evangelical affiliation. As in 2016, evangelical Black women were again more likely to support the Republican candidate in 2020, holding all other factors con-stant. In contrast, older Black women voters were more likely to support the Democratic candidate compared to younger voters. This comparison across election years shows that the types of Black women who vote for

Republican candidates vary only slightly across candidate contests. In both election years, only two factors differentiated Black women Democratic voters from Republican voters. The lack of distinguishing features of Black women Republican voters is because this is such a small subgroup relative to Black women Democratic voters.

Another important insight from this analysis is that factors often associated with Republican support among white women voters, such as living in the South or socioeconomic status, have no statistically significant impact on Black women's vote choice. For example, the majority of Black voters live in the South and nearly all Black women vote Democratic. Similarly, low-income voters make up the majority shares of both Black women Democratic and Republican voters. A systematic sorting of identity and interest groups into the two political parties is not occurring among Black women voters. This lack of systematic relationships between individual-level traits and vote choice for Black women voters demonstrates the constraints they have as a captured voting bloc within the Democratic Party.

While the demographic sorting into the two political parties is one way of understanding the constraint Black women experience at the voting booth, we also examine other indicators that reflect the relationship between constraint and partisan vote choice. Since we argue that the experiences of marginalization associated with both race and gender lead women of color to see the Democratic party as their only viable option at the voting booth, we expect that at the individual level, perceptions of racial and gendered marginalization correspond with stronger support for Democratic candidates.

To measure perceptions of racial and gendered marginalization, we can use survey items that ask respondents to rate the level of discrimination faced by African Americans and by women in society. By asking Black women respondents to rate discrimination against racial groups or against women, we can understand the extent to which they believe there exists systemic mistreatment due to race or gender. We anticipate that those Black women respondents who report facing significant discrimination are those who see race and gender to constrain one's life chances. Therefore, we anticipate that there should be a positive relationship between the belief that there is a lot of discrimination and vote for Democratic candidates.

Using data from the 2020 election, we find that the overwhelming majority (88%) of Black women believe there to be "a lot" of discrimination facing Black Americans while 47% of Black women strongly disagreed with a statement that

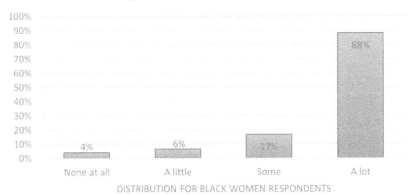

Figure 7 Black women's attitudes toward discrimination
against Blacks in 2020

Source: 2020 CMPS

discrimination against women is no longer a problem (see Figures 7 and 8). Only a small share of Black women claim there to be no discrimination toward either group (4% believe there to be no discrimination against Blacks and 5% strongly agreed that discrimination against women is no longer a problem). These data show how Black women as a group understand that race and gender constrains their life chances.

When we examine the relationship between perceived discrimination and Democratic vote choice in Figure 9, we see that among those Black women voters who perceive a lot of discrimination against Blacks, 95% voted for the Democratic candidate in 2020. In contrast, 83% of those who perceive no discrimination against Blacks voted for the Democratic candidate. Similarly, among those Black women respondents who strongly disagreed that discrimination against women is no longer a problem, 96% voted for the Democratic candidate. In contrast, 86% of those strongly agreed that discrimination against women is a problem for the Democratic candidate.[12] We do find variation in Democratic vote choice by discrimination attitudes.

This analysis shows that although Black women are a diverse population in terms of individual level demographics, they are nevertheless overwhelmingly

---

[12] Logistic regression confirms these relationships hold even when taking into account relevant controls. See Online Appendix Table A3.8.

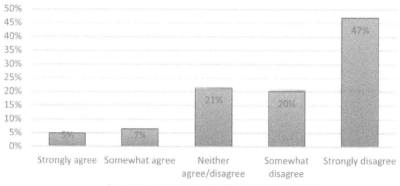

Figure 8 Black women's attitudes toward discrimination
against women in 2020

Source: 2020 CMPS

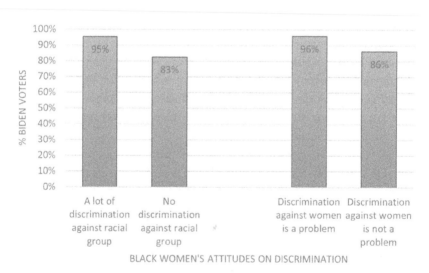

Figure 9 Relationship between attitudes toward discrimination and Democratic
vote for Black women voters in 2020

Source: 2020 CMPS

Democratic voters. In this way, their experiences rooted in their intersectional
race and gender position are of primary importance to their partisan candidate
vote choices. Our analysis shows that Black women do not sort into two parties
based on their individual-level traits or interests because they are constrained in

their agency of vote choice. Black women also generally hold attitudes that reflect their awareness and belief that their race and gender pose severe constraints on their life chances, which also correspond strongly with their partisan vote choice.

Latina Women Voters

In 2016 82% and in 2020 75% of Latina voters cast a ballot for the Democratic candidate (see Figure 6). So while strong majorities of Latinas support for Democratic candidates, more of these voters than Black women cast a ballot for Trump in 2016 and 2020. To test the extent to which there is systematic sorting by identity and interest groups that characterizes Latina voting patterns, we provide data on the demographic breakdown of Democratic and Republican Latina women voters in these two elections in Table 4. Bolded numbers reflect statistically significant differences. The data do not show a clear consistent pattern in the demographic makeup of Latina women Democratic and Republican, and there are fewer differences across individual-level factors in 2016 compared to 2020.

Using logistic regression analysis, we further confirm which factors differentiate Latina Democratic from Republican voters (for full results see Online Appendix Table A3.5). In 2016, we find that immigration-related factors and religion differentiated Latina Democratic and Republican voters. In contrast, in 2020 there were differences across age, income, national origin, immigration status, and religiosity between Latina Democratic and Republican voters. In 2020, those of higher income, of Cuban national origin, evangelical, and the highly religious were more likely to vote Republican. In contrast, those who identify as LGBTQ were more likely to vote for the Democratic candidate. It is notable that there are distinctive differences in individual-level traits among Democratic and Republican Latina voters in 2020 but less so in 2016. It is possible that the 2020 election represented a more typical American national election characterized as a contest between two white male candidates, despite the unique context of the pandemic. When voting in 2020, Latina voters' individual interests may have played a stronger role in determining their vote choice. Alternatively, it could be that in 2016, Latinas perceived more constraints on their vote choice given that gender was a more relevant factor with Clinton on the ballot.

One interesting pattern we find in this analysis are the findings for immigrant generation status. Although immigration from Latin American countries was a core issue discussed by candidates in 2016 and 2020 (Wallace and Zepeda Millan 2020), we find that there is no significant difference in the share of

Table 4 Demographics of Democratic and Republican Latina women voters in 2016 and 2020

	2016		2020	
	Clinton voters	**Trump voters**	**Biden voters**	**Trump voters**
Share of Latina voters	85	15	77	23
Age				
% Under 30	18	15	**13**	**6**
% Over 64	19	23	17	23
Socioeconomic status				
% HS degree or less	34	29	33	28
% College degree	25	29	31	33
% HH Income <$50 k	52	52	**49**	**41**
% HH Income >100 K	11	13	**14**	**21**
% Employed	38	31	37	42
Immigration				
% Foreign born	37	29	28	36
% Second gen[1]	**26**	**14**	**24**	**18**
% Third gen or more	**38**	**57**	44	44
National origin				
% Mexican	56	52	54	51
% Puerto Rican	**16**	**7**	**19**	**13**
% Cuban	3	6	**3**	**9**
Family Structure				
% Married	48	56	**48**	**65**
% Single/Never married	26	23	**25**	**15**
% Children in HH	70	76	33	37
US Region				
% Lives in South	34	44	**36**	**45**
Religion				
% Evangelical	**18**	**43**	9	20
% High Church Attend	**20**	**36**	28	45
Identity				
% LGBQ	7	5	**8**	**1**

Sources: 2016 and 2020 CMPS

Notes: Percentages are rounded to the nearest whole number. Data were weighted to align with the population estimates calculated from 2019 ACS. Bolded cells reflect statistically significant differences between Democratic and Republican voters at p<0.05
[1] 2nd generation=born in the United States with foreign-born parents; 3rd generation +=born in the United States with at least one US-born parent.

immigrant voters who make up Democratic and Republican Latina voters. In contrast, we find a distinct pattern for the second-generation (children of two immigrant parents) voters and those in their third generation (at least one parent is born in the United States) and beyond. Latinas in their third generation or beyond made up the majority of Republican Latina voters in 2016. Second-generation voters made up a larger share of Democratic Latina voters compared to that found among Republican Latina voters in both 2016 and 2020. This suggests that being a child of immigrants leads Latinas toward greater support of Democratic Party candidates, while Latinas whose families have been in the United States for more generations are more favorable to Republican Party candidates.

While we find that Latina voters display greater agency of choice in partisan candidate choice compared to Black women, it is still the case that those who perceive strong constraints of race and gender support Democratic candidates. Turning to attitudes on racial and gender discrimination, we find that a sizeable share, 42% of Latina respondents in 2020, perceived there to be a lot of discrimination against Latinos and 28% strongly disagreed with the idea that discrimination against women is no longer a problem (see Figures 10 and 11). As a whole, a large share of Latinas agree that race and gender pose severe constraints, but at the same time Latinas are less likely to perceive discrimination against their ethnic group or against women compared to Black women voters.

In addition, Latinas who perceive a lot of discrimination against Latinos or against women are more likely to vote for the Democratic candidate than those who perceive no discrimination.[13] As seen in Figure 12, there is a distinct contrast between the share of Biden voters among Latinas who perceive discrimination against Latinos or against women compared to those who do not perceive discrimination. Strikingly, an overwhelming majority (89%) of those who perceive a lot of discrimination against Latinos voted for Biden, whereas only 30% of those who perceive no discrimination against Latinos did so. Compared to what we found for Black women respondents, there is a stronger correspondence between individual attitudes about discrimination and vote choice. Perceptions of the constraints imposed by race or gender thus represent important predictors for Democratic vote choice among Latinas.

We find that the US presidential elections in this analysis mobilized distinct Latina electorates, and this variation suggests that Latina voters do perceive that

---

[13] Relationships continue to hold even when controlling for other relevant factors; see Online Appendix Table A3.8.

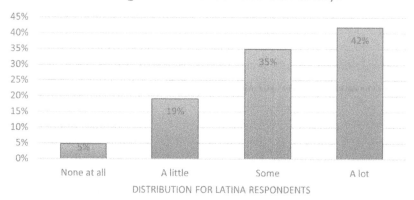

Figure 10 Latina attitudes toward discrimination against Latinos in 2020
Source: 2020 CMPS

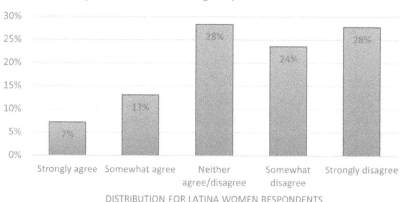

Figure 11 Latina attitudes toward discrimination against women in 2020
Source: 2020 CMPS

they hold agency in vote choice. Candidates and political parties can emphasize certain issues or agendas that generate support from different subgroups of Latina voters. Thus, Latina voters are less of a captured vote in the Democratic Party relative to Black women voters, though they are more constrained in their agency to choose than are white women voters.

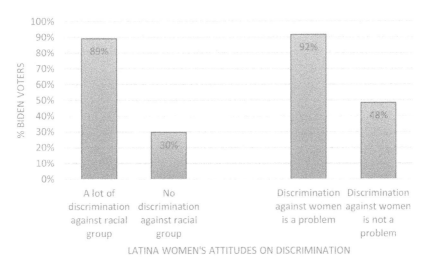

Figure 12 Relationship between attitudes toward discrimination and vote choice among Latina voters in 2020

Source: 2020 CMPS

Asian American Women Voters

Like Latinas, Asian American women demonstrate a stronger preference for Democratic candidates but at the same time reflect more heterogeneous attitudes compared to African American women. In 2016 79% and in 2020 72% of Asian American women voted for the Democratic candidate (see Figure 6). Relative to the other two women of color groups, Asian Americans demonstrate the widest variety in partisan vote choice all while being strongly supportive of Democrats.

Table 5 reports the demographic makeup of Asian American women voters who supported Democrats and Republicans in the two most recent presidential elections. In this analysis, we examine the same individual traits as for Latinas but include one additional variable, non-Christian religious affiliation, given that there is greater religious diversity within Asian Americans. We find there to be systematic variation in the individual-level traits between these two groups in both elections. We also find different patterns for 2016 than we do for 2020, demonstrating that each presidential race has mobilized different groups of Asian American voters. These results show that rather than demonstrating a stark pattern of captured voters, different subgroups of Asian American voters chose to cast their ballot for the candidate who best addresses their identities and interests in each election.

Table 5 Demographics of Democratic and Republican Asian American women
voters in 2016 and 2020

	2016		2020	
	Clinton voters	**Trump voters**	**Biden voters**	**Trump voters**
Makeup of Asian women voters	82	18	74	26
Age				
% Under 30	**9**	**2**	**11**	**3**
% Over 64	20	20	19	22
Socioeconomic status				
% HS degree or less	15	22	9	18
% College degree	66	60	69	60
% HH Income <$50 k	**26**	**12**	23	25
% HH Income >100 K	**35**	**56**	45	36
% Employed	46	49	46	41
Immigration				
% Foreign-born	**66**	**79**	**61**	**74**
% Second gen[1]	**21**	**10**	25	14
% Third gen or more	13	11	14	11
National origin				
% Chinese	27	26	31	31
% Indian	16	8	**18**	**10**
% Filipino	15	22	13	22
% Japanese	8	8	7	5
% Korean	**11**	**5**	10	8
% Vietnamese	10	19	8	12
Family Structure				
% Married	62	77	**60**	**69**
% Single/Never married	**22**	**7**	20	14
% Children in HH	**66**	**83**	30	30
US Region				
% Lives in South	23	29	**23**	**34**
Religion				
% Evangelical	**14**	**29**	**4**	**18**
% High Church Attend	**14**	**34**	20	43
% Non-Christian	**26**	**13**	36	25

Table 5 (cont.)

	2016		2020	
	Clinton voters	**Trump voters**	**Biden voters**	**Trump voters**
Identity				
% LGBQ	5	6	**5**	**2**

Sources: 2016 and 2020 CMPS

Notes: Percentages are rounded to the nearest whole number. Data were weighted to align with the population estimates calculated from 2019 ACS. Bolded cells reflect statistically significant differences between Democratic and Republican voters at p<0.05.

[1] 2nd generation=born in the United States with foreign-born parents; 3rd generation +=born in the United States with at least one US-born parent.

Results from multivariate analyses show that in 2016, Asian American women who were single, US-born, and Korean were more likely to support the Democratic Party candidate, while those who identified as evangelical were more likely to support the Republican candidate. In 2020, those who were older, lived in the southern states, and identified as evangelical were more likely vote Republican, whereas those who identified as lesbian, gay, or bisexual were more likely to vote Democratic (see Online Appendix Table A3.7).

One factor noteworthy about this analysis of Asian American women is the lack of national origin variation explaining partisan vote choice. Our analysis of national origin variation uses Chinese Americans as the comparison group (which represents the largest national origin group among Asian Americans). Chinese Americans are also the group least likely to identify as a strong partisan, thus making it an appropriate comparison group for analysis (Wong et al. 2011; Masuoka et al. 2018). Analyses that include all Asian Americans find that Vietnamese Americans are more likely to identify as Republican relative to other groups (Lien, Conway, and Wong 2004; Wong et al. 2011). But this analysis focusing only on Asian American women does not show this same pattern. In contrast, we find that in 2016 there is only one significant difference between Korean women (relative to Chinese women). Furthermore, there were no significant national origin differences in 2020 among South Asian Indians despite the fact that Kamala Harris ran as Vice President on the Democratic Party ticket (but see Lemi, Arora, and Sadhwani 2020). It is possible that national origin differences are driven by Asian

American men or within the broader Asian American population that includes non-voters.

Turning to perceptions of discrimination among Asian American women, 29% believe there to be a lot of discrimination against Asian Americans, but an even larger share (41%) of Asian American women report there to be "some" discrimination against Asian Americans in 2020 (see Figure 13). Similarly on the gender discrimination question, we find that a sizeable share of Asian American women respondents hold more moderate attitudes compared to African American women voters. Thirty percent strongly disagree that discrimination against women is no longer a problem, but 28% reported to neither agree nor disagree (see Figure 14). Among Asian American women voters, those with more moderate attitudes on discrimination make up a large share of the group. It is possible that these voters perceive discrimination consistent with the societal racialization of Asian American women where their racial group of Asian is seen as more privileged compared to Blacks and Latinos. Finally, a relatively smaller share of Asian American women voters perceive there to be significant discrimination compared to what we found for Black women respondents, and the pattern perceptions of gender discrimination attitudes are similar to Latina voters.

There is a correspondence between discrimination attitudes and Democratic vote choice in 2020 for Asian American women (see Figure 15). Among Asian American women who perceive there to be a lot of discrimination against Asian Americans, 86% voted for Biden, while for those who perceive there to be no discrimination against Asian Americans, the rate was 46%. We find a similar pattern on attitudes toward discrimination against women.[14]

The variation in individual-level predictors of partisan vote choice across elections demonstrates that Asian American women perceive that they hold more agency in vote choice compared to African American women voters who experience the strongest intersectional constraint. The racial tropes that stereotype Asian Americans have both positive and negative valances (i.e., "model minority" and "foreign outsider"), and as such, Asian American women may perceive racial discrimination as less of a problem than other minority women. Therefore, consistent with their racialization, Asian American women demonstrate more variation in their vote choice compared to Black and Latina women voters.

---

[14] These relationships continue to hold even when controlling for other relevant factors. See Online Appendix Table A3.8.

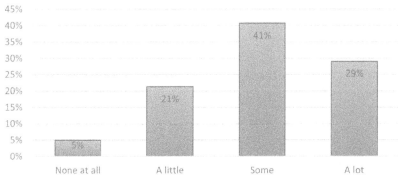

Figure 13 Asian American women's attitudes about discrimination against Asian Americans in 2020

Source: 2020 CMPS

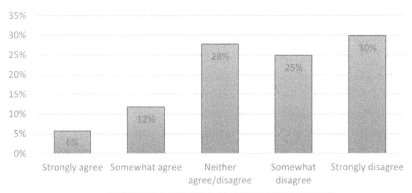

Figure 14 Asian American women's attitudes about discrimination against women in 2020

Source: 2020 CMPS

Discussion

The descriptor "women of color" is an all-encompassing term of relatively recent vintage, with much of its meaning relevant to differentiating women by race and ethnicity. By asserting this distinction, women of color emphasize their

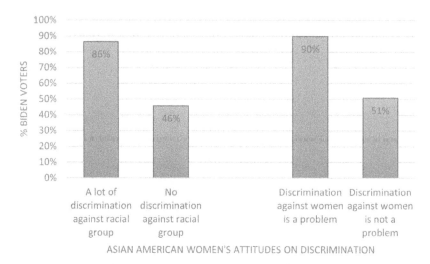

Figure 15 Relationship between attitudes toward discrimination and vote
choice among Asian American voters in 2020

Source: 2020 CMPS

intersectional experience as being simultaneously racialized as non-white and
distinct from the "default category" political subject as women. The analysis in
this section demonstrates that this intersectional experience leads women of
color to embrace progressive political positions and be stronger political supporters of candidates representing the Democratic Party. Women of color
remain the stalwart of the modern Democratic Party and support their candidates by wide margins in US presidential politics.

Nevertheless, women of color voters have been taken for granted and
ignored by political parties and analysts alike, and are not ordinarily the
subject of systematic or sustained study. This needs to change, and the
empirical analysis presented in this section provides the basis for a clearer
picture of the politically relevant traits of Black, Latina, and Asian American
women voters. While characteristics such as educational attainment and
marital status have often been marshalled by political commentators to
explain why women voters supported Trump in 2016 and 2020, our analysis
shows that these arguments are less applicable to the partisan candidate
choices of women of color. As argued at the outset of the section, all
women of color are not the same, and instead, the analysis reveals
a different degree of constraint by race, with Black women voters the most
"captured" by the Democratic Party, followed by Latinas and then Asian
Americans.

Taken together, this analysis and these results instantiate an intersectional analytical approach to explaining partisan vote choice in US presidential elections. While women of color cast ballots heavily in favor of Democratic Party candidates, this degree of support is based on both the issue positions of voters and more progressive candidates while simultaneously being a reflection of the intersectional position of non-white women voters as "captured" voters. To the extent that one of the two major political parties espouses policies to support the status quo marginalization of women and minorities, women of color have constrained agency in partisan candidate choice.

4 The Diverse Politics of White Women Voters

The outcome of 2016 US presidential election was set in sharp relief to pre-election horserace polls that showed a wide and positive gender gap of women voters compared to men favoring the Democrat. But for Clinton supporters, instead of election night 2016 being the night women would flex their political muscle in a woman candidate's favor, it was, in fact, another instance when white women voters evinced their power with a majority casting their ballots for Trump. Two days later, *The New York Times* published an opinion piece entitled "White Women Voted Trump. Now What?" where the author appealed to white women to see connections in their interests across race, sexuality, and class (Lett 2016).

That said, it is inaccurate to claim that white women are overwhelmingly Republican. They are not, and while a similar proportion of white women voters would support Trump in his quest for re-election four years later, this pattern should not obscure the fact that though a smaller proportion of white women voted for the Democratic Party candidates, they made up the biggest portion of Democratic voters in both the 2016 and 2020 presidential races. Both of these facts are true at the same time, and reflect the reality that white women voters are the most heterogeneous among women voters in terms of partisan candidate choice. Nevertheless, the power of confirmation bias rooted in the gender gap narrative and supported by the fact that women voters in the aggregate are Democratic made the conditions right for commentators to assume that white women would behave in the same way as women overall.

In this section we take a closer look at white women voters, illuminating the traits that separate Democratic versus Republican supporters among them. The reality that white women voters are heterogeneous in their political preferences has been underexplored, and as a result, there is less systematic knowledge about the reasons that propel their support for Republican or Democratic Party candidates and estimate inferential models utilizing ANES data over the last four presidential elections.

Diverse White Women Voters: Feminists, Working Moms, and (Still) Suburban Warriors

In addition to the presence of the gender gap, the abiding impression that white women voters are more Democratic than Republican is aided by two trends: the increasing national visibility of Democratic women elected officials and the transition of feminist beliefs into the political mainstream. The year 1992 was called the "year of the woman" in politics, a moniker intended to herald the election of a record number of women US senators. This feat enhanced the previous gender balance from 98 men and 2 women, to 93 men and 7 women seated in the Senate chamber of the 103rd Congress. Progress no doubt, but the pronouncement that a woman's place was "in the House and the Senate" remained a hopeful feminist slogan rather than a reality. Five out of six of those newly elected women senators were Democrats, helping to solidify the perception that women were politically Democratic. Equally important, of the seven women US senators in 1993, all but one was white, and gender politics at the national level was still dominated by white women.

Alongside the growth of white women elected officials, there were also visible white feminist activists of the "second wave" generation who advocated for equality in politics, at home, in society, and in the workplace (Klein 1984). Almost two decades after the Equal Rights Amendment (ERA) failed to be ratified as a constitutional amendment, the feminist movement of mid-century had grown into the mainstream by the "year of the woman." Younger women of a new generation had substantially more reproductive freedom than their mothers and grandmothers, and were able to access higher education and, concomitantly, a broader set of employment opportunities. Together these developments provided the context that explained why some white women voters cast their support for Democrats and are credited with creating the gender gap in preference for Democrats. But, of course, this is only part of the story.

Despite progressive change supporting greater equality for women in American society, conservative white women who believe in traditional gender roles and support Republican Party policies and candidates remain ever present though with a smaller imprint on the collective imagination compared to progressive and feminist politicians. The common – and erroneous – portrayal of white women voters as majority supporters of Democrats is a reflection of greater public attention to those white women who choose to reject patriarchal constraints, compared to white women conservatives who abide the normalization of traditional gender roles. Derisive characterizations of liberal white women are commonplace, from candidate Trump labeling his opponent a "nasty woman" to Republican US Senate Majority Leader Mitch McConnell shaming Senator Elizabeth Warren for continuing to speak ("nevertheless she persisted"). Within conservative political rhetoric, those who challenge a patriarchal worldview of appropriate behavior for women receive more attention than those who toe the line of traditional gendered behavior. In this area of the culture wars around sex and gender, analysts have overlooked the substantial political diversity and indeed the dominance of conservative and Republican Party supporters among white women voters in the United States.

Conservative women in politics have been present and politically influential since at least the time white women were granted the franchise (see also Jacobs 2014). Take, for example, Phyllis Schlafly, the conservative activist whose opposition to the ERA – marketed with catchy red octagonal signs emblazoned with "S.T.O.P." (stop taking our privileges) – remains deeply rooted among white women voters (Critchlow 2008). Schlafly's reference to privileges included being protected and cherished, and as such required the embrace of marriage and motherhood. But Schlafly is not the only example of influential white women in conservative politics. Scholars have detailed political leadership among Republican white women at different times of the conservative movement, and in her book *Suburban Warriors*, historian Lisa McGirr identified conservative white women activists in Orange County, California, in the early 1960s as among the originators of the "new American right" by cultivating politics that fused traditional Western liberalism with xenophobia and Christian fundamentalism (McGirr 2011). Indeed, Schlafly and other conservative white women suburban warriors of this era helped to forge the rhetoric and the playbook of modern conservative women, their legacy is clearly audible in contemporary efforts such as reproductive rights and advocacy for charter schools (Rymph 2006). Just as importantly, conservative white women did not limit their politics to only gendered issues and have been involved in early efforts opposing universal suffrage (Goodie 2012) and upholding formal practices of Jim Crow (Love 2016; McRae 2018; Darby 2020).

White women voters overall reflect a diverse electorate that, while stereotyped as liberal and Democratic in their politics, are instead more conservative and Republican.

A Dynamic Electorate: Agency in Vote Choice
for White Women Voters

Analyzing the diversity of the white women electorate in US presidential elections yields the fundamental fact that despite majority Republican Party candidate support among women, there remains a strong subset of this electorate that votes Democratic. Indeed, and because white women are the biggest slice of the pie within the American electorate, they are also the largest group of supporters for both Republican and Democratic Party candidates. Looking at 2016, for example, white women represented 32% of all Democratic voters and 45% of all Republican voters. Moreover, white women outnumber white men in both parties. White men represented only 26% of Democratic voters and 42% of Republican voters in 2016. Given that women are more likely to turn out to vote compared to men, white women represent a critical voting bloc for both Democrats and Republicans. Understanding the dynamics of white women voters is therefore crucial to unraveling the factors and reasons for candidate choice among this powerful group in the electorate.

At the same time, we point to the power and privilege white women voters hold in American elections. We argue that white women are understood overall as a powerful voting bloc and a core electoral base of both the Democratic and Republican parties. Unlike women of color who experience party capture and vote primarily for Democrats, white women are seen as important electorates to be cultivated by candidates and sometimes can be potentially lured to cross party lines. White women voters cast their ballots for parties and candidates who run on platforms that appeal to their interests and stances on political issues, and this is no different from what we expect of white men voters.

In this way, white women represent the group of women voters who hold the highest degree of agency in vote choice during presidential elections. Because white women voters can cast their ballot for the candidate or party that best addresses their identities and interests, we expect there to be systematic variation in the demographic makeup of white women Democratic voters compared to that of their Republican counterparts in each election. At the same time, because social, economic, and political norms are dynamic, we expect that the variation that exists among white women voters will vary across time and election context. We thus also expect that the factors predicting either Democratic or Republican vote choice for white women voters will vary in each election. The fact that it can change is a further reflection of their agency in vote choice.

Data and Methods

For this analysis, we utilize data from the 2008, 2012, 2016, and 2020 ANES post-election data. The ANES represents the ideal survey data for this analysis of white women voters over multiple elections given that the dataset includes a consistent set of survey items for every presidential election since 1948. While surveys like the CMPS offer large oversamples of racial minority respondents to identify variation within each minority group, the ANES provides a nationally representative sample of white voters. We caution that these data do not allow us to analyze at the individual level if voters change their opinions across elections since it is not a panel study design. Rather, it provides information about the traits among white women electorates supporting Democratic or Republican Party candidates for each election. Through a comparison of elections we can draw useful insights to show if, for example, Republican candidates across elections attract similar types of white women voters across elections or if they vary by election. The analysis provides evidence as to the extent to which white women voters are strong partisans who vote for the same party across elections or if they shift their support in response to particular candidates and platforms.[15]

We selected the most recent four elections (2008–2020) given that within this set there were a number of historic firsts such as the opportunity to elect the first Black president, the first woman Republican Party vice president, the first woman president, and the first Black and Asian vice president. In addition, both 2008 and 2016 were considered relatively competitive contests since the party nominees did not include an incumbent and research shows that more voters are more likely to be engaged when the contest is competitive (Grofman, Collet, and Griffin 1998). As in in the previous section, we present factors commonly identified as being related to partisan candidate choice.

Who Are White Women Democratic Voters and Who Are White Women Republican Voters?

Table 6 presents the characteristics of white women Democratic and Republican electorates in each presidential election between 2008 and 2020.[16] The percentages report the demographic characteristics of white women Democratic voters and Republican voters as well as a difference of proportion. Statistically significant differences are highlighted in bold in the table. For example, in

---

[15] There are many other surveys that ask about voting with validating voter turnout. However, ANES is the main study that offers a consistent set of questions asked in each election.

[16] See Online Appendix B for survey items.

Table 6 Demographic makeup of Democratic and Republican white women voters

	2008		2012		2016		2020	
	Obama voters	McCain voters	Obama voters	Romney voters	Clinton voters	Trump voters	Biden voters	Trump voters
% Makeup of White Women	45	53	44	54	41	53	44	55
Age								
% Under 30	23	12	15	11	15	11	18	11
% Over 64	19	23	24	27	23	30	26	21
Socioeconomic status								
% HS degree or less	35	33	31	37	18	34	18	35
% College degree	37	36	39	31	57	29	56	31
% HH Income <$50 k	54	41	41	40	30	42	17	17
% HH Income >100 K	15	19	26	19	38	23	57	53
% Employed	65	63	48	46	64	48	58	59
Family Structure								
% Married	47	63	47	70	58	67	56	63
% Never married	25	12	24	9	21	12	22	17

% Children in HH[1]	32	39	28	33	30	30	31	30
% Lives in South[2]	**30**	**55**	**23**	**38**	**24**	**41.6**	**27**	**44**
Religion								
% Evangelical[3]	**23**	**58**	**10**	**28**	**8**	**25**	**6**	**27**
% High Church Attend	**16**	**46**	**15**	**34**	**9**	**33**	**14**	**39**
Group membership								
% labor union HH	**15**	**9**	**23**	**16**	**21**	**13**	**18**	**14**
% armed forces	3	3	1	3	2	2	1	4
Identity								
% LGBQ	**12**	**2**	**5**	**1**	**10**	**2**	**9**	**1**

Sources: ANES Cumulative File, 2008, 2012, 2016, and 2020 Time Series

Note: Numbers are rounded to the nearest whole number. Bolded entries reflect the difference between Democratic and Republican voters in a given election to be statistically significant at p<0.5.

[1] The question wording for children in the household varies across surveys. See Online Appendix B.

[2] Measures of the respondent's location varies across surveys. See Online Appendix B.

[3] The question wording to measure religious affiliation varies across surveys. See Online Appendix B.

2008, 35% of white women Obama voters held no more than a high school level of education and 37% of white women Obama voters were college educated. However, there are no significant differences in the distribution of education among white women Democrat versus Republican voters in 2008. In contrast, in 2016 and 2020, white women Democratic voters were more likely to be college-educated compared to Republican voters. We present a visualization of these differences in Figure 16.

There is also consistency in the religious affiliation, sexual orientation, and regional makeup of white women Democratic and Republican voters across elections. In terms of regional makeup, Republican supporters are a third or more composed of voters from southern states. For example, white women Republican supporters in 2008 were heavily represented by southern women, with 55% that election year living in that region. This is in contrast to the 30% of the sample of white women who voted for Obama in 2008 that lived in the south. We note that the data take an interesting turn over time, however, with much smaller proportions of both supporters of Republicans and Democrats residing in the south. This suggests that overall, white women electorates are becoming more dispersed in terms of residence across the United States.

In terms of religion, the data show that at least a third of Republican white women voters are highly religious (as measured by church attendance rates) and a good share identify as evangelical or born-again Christian. We acknowledge that the distinct difference between the share of religious voters in 2008 compared to other election years might be due to differences in question wording across surveys rather than changes in the makeup of electorates over time.[17]

A third characteristic of which we find there to be statistically significant differences across Democratic and Republican white women voters is the makeup in terms of sexual orientation. Those who identify as lesbian, bisexual, or other make up a small share of the overall population, but they comprise a larger share of white women Democratic voters compared to white women Republican voters. This finding on is important as it demonstrates how white women voters can be responsive to party cues that speak to a marginalized status. Like the political stances made on behalf of racial and gender equality, the Democratic Party has over recent election cycles taken a clear political stance supporting gay marriage and LGBT+ rights.

---

[17] In 2008 and 2020, respondents were asked a distinct question if they were "born-again" or had a conversion experience. In 2012 and 2016, evangelical was provided by the respondent when asked about their religious affiliation.

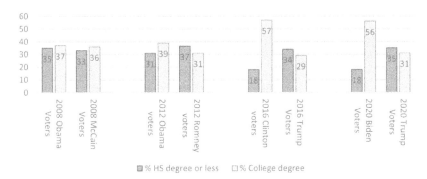

Figure 16 Educational makeup of white women Democratic and Republican voters 2008, 2012, 2016, and 2020

Source: ANES 2008, 2012, 2016, and 2020 Time Series

While there were some consistent patterns across elections, more notable are the differences across electorates on the demographic factors analyzed. In terms of age, white women Democratic voters on average are a few years younger on than their Republican counterparts, though the difference is not large. When looking at specific age groups, in 2008 and 2020, younger white women voters made up a larger share of Democratic voters than their makeup of Republican voters. In 2016, older voters (those 65 years or older) made up 30% of Trump voters compared to the 23% of Clinton voters. This shows that some age groups were more mobilized to support specific presidential candidates in certain contests.

The most striking finding, however, is the absence of a strong pattern of Republican Party or Democratic Party candidate support by socioeconomic status across election years. In particular, each shows different compositions of income categories among voters for each party's candidates. Using household income as a measure, Democratic-supporting white women voters were composed more of lower income voters in 2008. By 2016, however, it is Republican white women who have a larger representation among lower-income voters within Trump's coalition that year. For instance, in 2008, an estimated 54% of Democratic women voters had a household income of less than $50,000 a year, while in 2016 only 30% of Hillary Clinton's white women voters were in this income bracket. Interestingly, while there are significant differences on makeup by household income for 2008, 2012, and 2016, in 2020 there are not distinctive differences in income level between Democratic and Republican voters.

Similarly, and in terms of educational attainment, data from 2008 show no significant differences between Democratic and Republican white women voters. An almost identical proportion of Obama supporters had high school as their highest attainment, as did Republican white women voters. Similarly, there is a near-perfect match in proportion with a college degree in 2008 for both the Democratic and Republican candidate coalitions. But since 2012, college-educated voters make up a larger share of Democratic voters compared to Republican voters. In 2016 and 2020, there are big differences between Clinton and Trump voters, with over half of Democratic voters holding a college degree (57% in 2016 and 56% in 2020).

Finally, and in terms of family structure, married women make up a large share of both parties but represent a larger share of Republican white women voters across the presidential elections between 2008 and 2020. In contrast, women who have never married make up over one fifth of Democratic voters across all four elections. We do not find any significant differences in the makeup of women with children in the household across the two parties.

Predicting Republican Support across the Last Four Presidential Elections

The analysis in the previous section helped to form a picture of the white women electorate and what differentiates Democratic versus Republican voters. However, it is possible that demographic factors may be correlated with one another. For example, it could be the case that southern voters are more likely to be older or married and so we would need to account for the possibility that regional location has a distinct impact on partisan vote choice from that of age and marital status. To ascertain if there are factors that have a systematic impact on partisan candidate choice we turned to multivariate analyses.

Since more white women voters prefer Republican candidates, for this analysis we specified a logistic regression model predicting vote choice for the Republican candidate (compared to vote for a Democratic candidate).[18] For independent variables, we tested for the same demographic characteristics analyzed in the previously. Given that we use a logistic regression, the coefficients for each independent variable are not easily comparable across one another. To compare the magnitude of each coefficient with that of each of the others in the model, we also calculate log odds for each independent variable in the model. For log odds, values greater than 1 demonstrate that the independent variable has a positive effect on the dependent variable with larger numbers reporting there to be a stronger magnitude. Values between 0 and 1 demonstrate

---

[18] We excluded those who voted for a third party in this analysis.

that the independent variable has a negative effect on the dependent variable, with values closer to 0 reflecting a stronger (negative) magnitude of an effect. For ease of interpretation we only present significant results in Table 7.[19]

The results from the multivariate analyses show that there are some factors that have a unique impact predicting Republican candidate choice among white women. Yet, just like the demographic analysis, we find that there are not consistent predictors when we compare results across presidential elections between 2008 and 2020. This tells us that white women who vote Republican are not necessarily comprised of the same population across elections. However, we do find some factors that are significant predictors across elections, for example, being an evangelical Christian and living in the South both predict Republican vote choice among white women. Identifying as LGBT+ is the one variable that consistently predicts Democratic vote choice among white women.

The results from these analyses reveal that if we want to characterize the partisan candidate choices of white women voters, one way to describe them is as swing voters. Systematically examining the factors that predict partisan candidate choice across four presidential elections shows that while there are some demographic differences in the makeup of Democratic and Republican white women voters, this absence of consistent patterns of partisan support – with the exception of living in the south, religiosity, and sexual orientation – demonstrates changing electorates in each election. One conclusion from the findings of the absence of level of education or marital status or even income having consistent effects over time among white women in their partisan candidate choices is that white women voters are both dynamic and heterogeneous. Differences in the context, candidates and other time-specific factors found in each election affect the vote choice of white women voters, giving credence to the truism that every election has a distinct electorate.

Discussion

The fact that white women voters are more evenly split in their partisan candidate choices for US president underscores both the broader agency of white women to choose between the political parties and their electoral power in choosing the President of the United States. Constrained as they are by their gender, in terms of the positions the two major political parties take on traditional gender roles and accompanying policies on gender equity, white women nevertheless can and do choose between the

---

[19] See Online Appendix A Table A4.1 for full models.

Table 7 Factors that predict support for the Republican candidate among white women voters: 2008, 2012, 2016, and 2020

	2008 Vote for McCain		2012 Vote for Romney		2016 Vote for Trump		2020 Vote for Trump	
	b (s.e.)	Odds ratio	b (s.e.)	Odds ratio	b (s.e.)	Odds ratio	b (s.e.)	Odds ratio
Age								
Income	.07 (.03)	1.1**						
Education			−.18 (.08)	.83*	−.60 (.10)	.55**	−.60 (.08)	.55**
Never married			−1.1 (.24)	.33**				
Children in HH								
Employed								
Evangelical	1.0 (.30)	2.9**	1.0 (.23)	2.7**			1.0 (.31)	2.7**
Church attend	.17 (.08)	1.2*	.37 (.05)	1.4**	.29 (.05)	1.3**	.31 (.04)	1.4**
Union					−.54 (.21)	.58*		
South	.81 (.26)	2.2**	.40 (.18)	1.5*	.71 (.18)	2.0**	.62 (.19)	1.9**
Military			1.37 (.48)	4.0**			1.8 (.65)	6.1**
LGBQ	−1.8 (.64)	.17**	−1.34 (.57)	.26*	−1.3 (.48)	.26**	−2.0 (.50)	.13**
Constant								
N	413		1213		910		1317	

Sources: ANES 2008, 2012, 2016, and 2020 Time Series

*p<0.05; **p<0.01

Notes: Logistic regression models using sampling weights.

two parties in a more evenly distributed fashion especially compared to women of color. In contrast, Black, Latina, Asian American, and other women of color give heavily lopsided support for Democratic Party candidates. Women of color do not have the same degree of agency to choose, for the policies of one of the parties constrain their realistic choices at the ballot. Together these patterns of partisan candidate choice among highly heterogeneous white women voters and constrained agency for women of color lay the groundwork for revealing the dynamics of the gender gap in the next section.

5 The Gender Gap Is a Race Gap

The concept of the gender gap – ordinarily defined as the difference between support among men and women voters for the winning candidate – was introduced to the American political lexicon in the 1980s when a pattern of stronger support of Democrats among women first emerged. When Democrats won, the gender gap was always positive sometimes 10 points or more, indicating that women voters were stronger supporters of Democratic Party candidates for president compared to men voters. Political commentators and election prognosticators often look to the gender gap before a contest to predict outcomes, and then after the election to explain what happened. Most often the interpretation leads to the presumption that women are Democratic voters and therefore will be a core electorate leading a Democratic candidate to victory.

What has been lost in the gender gap heuristic is the recognition that a gender gap favoring Democratic candidates among women voters can coexist with a pattern of majority support among some women voters for Republican Party candidates. Calculation of the gender gap presumes that sorting by gender and comparing women voters against men offers insight into the politics of women voters. This is true, but only part of the story. Once we acknowledge that women voters are a large and diverse group and focus instead on their internal heterogeneity in partisan candidate choice, we can learn much more about the political preferences of women voters. A disaggregation of the women electorate by race reveals that a majority of white women voters support Republican candidates and that their majority support of Republican candidates has been consistent over the same time during which the gender gap first appeared. The majority of white women voters supported Ronald Reagan in 1980 (54%) and in 1984 (62%), as well as George H.W. Bush in 1988 (59%). In contrast, women of color vote in the majority for Democratic candidates with black women in particular voting overwhelmingly Democrat for all years that we have available data.

In this section,[20] we show that the positive numbers overall for women supporting Democratic candidates are due to the rapid rise of women of color in the
electorate and their heavily lopsided support of Democratic Party nominees
(McClain, Carter, and Brady 2005; Bejarano 2014; Tien 2017). Together these
women of color voters and their strong support for Democrats have obscured the
consistent pattern of majority Republican support among white women. The
pattern of American women voting majority Democratic often leads to the inference that white women are more Democratic than they actually are. Thus, the
gender gap is a race gap inasmuch as it can be explained by the heterogeneous
behavior among women voters and in this case the fact that support for Democratic
Party candidates is differentiated by race.

All the same, we also will show that women voters are modestly more
supportive of Democratic Party candidates for president compared to men,
and that this pattern persists across white, Black, Latinx, and Asian American
voters. These data help to substantiate the claim that the political positions
staked out by the two parties are gendered as well as racialized.

Identifying and Explaining the Gender Gap

The narrative about women voters being stronger Democratic Party supporters
compared to men is based on a decades-long literature in political science
scholarship (Box-Steffensmeier, DeBoef, and Lin 2004; Whitaker 2008; Fox
and Carroll 2013). The longitudinal data presented in Figure 17 document the
gender gap over time for the entire series of ANES data between 1948 and 2020.
While there is variation over the nearly seventy years of US presidential election
data, the gender gap in the early years is negative, meaning women voters were
less supportive of Democrats compared to men prior to 1964. Since then, the
gender gap is positive and modest, usually in single digits with the exception of
the US presidential election years in the 1990s when Democrats Bill Clinton and
Al Gore were more popular with white women voters.

The elections of 1992, 1996, and 2000 were, if not unique in the history of
modern presidential contests, nevertheless different from other years since the
1980s because of the inclusion of third-party candidates who drew substantial
votes from the two major party candidates. Ross Perot ran in both 1992 and
1996, siphoning support from Republican Party nominees George H.W. Bush
and Robert Dole, and therefore inflating the size of the gender gap in those two
elections. In 2000, the candidacy of Ralph Nader drew voters from the opposite
end of the political spectrum. Overall, and taken together, the gender gap in
partisan candidate choice is visible and persistent.

---

[20] This section is developed from our previous work; see Junn and Masuoka 2020.

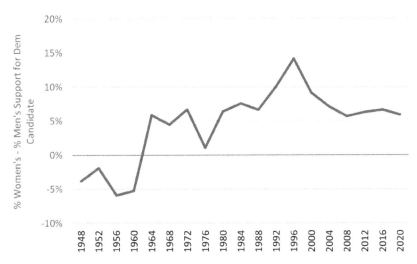

Figure 17 Gender gap difference between women's and men's support for
Democratic candidates, 1948–2020

Source: ANES Cumulative File, 1948–2020

Another way to look at the data is to track the preferred party candidate of
women and of men over time. Figure 18 presents the same data used to calculate
the gender gap in Figure 17, but instead of highlighting the difference between
men and women, it shows the share of women and of men who supported the
Democratic Party candidate in each presidential election. Until 1980, men
voters supported Democrats at a higher rate than women voters in some
elections and for others the reverse is true, and there is no discernible gender
and party phenomenon in the earlier years. In contrast, and starting in the 1980s,
the data show consistent majority support for Democratic Party nominees
among women. In sum, the conventional wisdom since the 1980s is that
women voters appear to be majority Democratic in their support of US presidential candidates, and also more Democratic than men voters.

Since the gender gap was identified, researchers have attempted to explain the
reasons for the variation. Academic studies narrowed in on gender differences on
policy issues such as social welfare (Howell and Day 2000), foreign policy
(Chaney, Alvarez, and Nagler 1998), abortion (Mansbridge 1986; Cook, Jelen,
and Wilcox 1993), economic attitudes (Welch and Hibbing 1992; Seltzer,
Newman, and Leighton 1997), and feminism (Conover 1988; Cook and Wilcox
1991) that were more consistent with progressive and Democratic Party positions.
The interpretation that developed into conventional wisdom is that women are
more politically liberal on issues compared to men due to their primary role as
caregivers and the experience of gendered stereotypes leading to a stronger

Figure 18 Percent support of Democratic Party candidates by gender,
1948–2020

Source: ANES Cumulative File, 1948–2020

feminist consciousness. Other scholars have argued that increased economic independence of women (Manza and Brooks 1998), the declining significance of traditional marriage (Iversen and Rosenbluth 2006), and increased educational opportunities for women (Gillion, Ladd, and Meredith 2020) explain the conditions under which the gender gap developed.

While most of the literature focuses on the distinctiveness of women's attitudes and the implications of those opinions for candidate choice, other scholars have pointed out that women's candidate choices and partisan identities have remained relatively stable over time. Instead, they interpret the gender gap as a reflection of the diminution of support among men for Democratic Party candidates for president (Kaufmann and Petrocik 1999). Alternatively, Box-Steffensmeier, De Boef, and Lin (2004) argue that fluctuations in the size of the gender gap are due to larger, macro-level factors such as the political climate (like public support for conservatism) and economic conditions (such as unemployment and inflation) since these factors influence the individual lives of men and women in systematically different ways (Ondercin 2017).

Taken together, this research points to the reaction of women to support a politics that challenges, rather than enhances, patriarchal dominance and inequality on the basis of gender. Important as this is for the study of electoral politics and candidate choice, the fact remains that while women voters have shown stronger support for Democratic Party candidates compared to men voters, there is far from uniformity among women.

The Gender Gap Is a Race Gap

The persistence of the gender gap in election results alongside the robust academic literature on the concept reinforces the widespread characterization of American women as Democratic Party supporters (Dittmar 2017). But the data do not support the argument that this is the modal position among *all* American women voters. Instead, the reliance on defining women's choices in comparison to those of men – as the default category from which all else deviates – is a flawed analytical position because it obscures the variation within women voters.

As the data[21] in Figure 19 demonstrate, the most striking difference in support for Democratic Party candidates within the population of women voters in the United States is race. White women voters are the least supportive of Democrats compared to African American women and Latina voters. While the data for Latinas in the ANES surveys are sparse for this fast-growing group of voters and most reliable from the election of 2008 and onward, the basic pattern among Latinas is instructive.[22] Black women are the strongest and most consistent supporters of Democratic Party candidates, followed by Latinas who also vote for Democratic nominees by a strong majority. In contrast, white women show the lowest support for Democratic Party candidates, consistently less than 50%, with only two exceptions

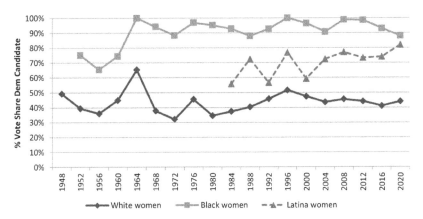

Figure 19 Percent support of Democratic Party presidential candidates by race, 1948–2020

Source: ANES Cumulative File, 1948–2020

---

[21] Figure uses ANES data since CMPS data only provide data for 2016 and 2020.
[22] Sample sizes provided in Online Appendix Table A5.1. There are too Asian American women respondents in ANES for reliable reporting.

in the years of 1964 and 1996 in majority support for Democrats. Rather than comparing women to men to generate the conventional gender gap number, comparing partisan candidate choice by race and ethnicity within the population of women voters reveals that not all women voters in US presidential elections are Democratic supporters. Instead, the gender gap is created by a race gap, with women of color leading the way.

Democratic Party support among African American women surpasses 90% in 1964 and then essentially never wavers. Black women consistently and overwhelmingly support Democratic candidates, and these voters are the stalwart of the Democratic Party in US presidential elections (Jordan-Zachary 2007). Support for Democratic candidates among Latinas is less consistent compared to African American women, particularly in the early elections between 1988 and 2000.[23] But since 2000, the data reveal a steady increase in Democratic Party candidate support among Latinas, never dropping below 70% in the last four elections. Although there are less data on Asian American women, surveys focusing on this population of voters show that Asian American women support Democratic candidates at a level similar to Latina voters. Explanations for the strong Democratic support among women of color have been discussed in a growing body of research and reflect the intersectional position of women of color as marginalized by both gender and race (Garcia Bedolla and Scola 2006; Hardy-Fanta et al. 2016).

Despite the wide variation between white women and women of color, there remains a partisan gender gap by race. Table 8 details the proportions who supported Democratic Party candidates for US president by gender and race/ethnicity during the last four elections.[24,25] Looking at the gender gap calculations, we find that there are differences in the size of the gap between women's preferences for Democratic Party candidates compared to men for all racial groups in all US presidential elections between 2008 and 2020.[26] The relatively modest sample sizes for women of color in the American National Election Study data caution one from drawing strong conclusions about the observed

---

[23] Early surveys in the ANES were only conducted in English and oversampling techniques were only employed on Black respondents. More recent bilingual surveys on Latinos confirm that Latinos are majority Democratic (see Fraga et al. 2011).

[24] We could not calculate reliable estimates of Asian American vote choice in the ANES and so utilized other surveys with more reliable Asian American data fielded since 2000. For this see Online Appendix Table A5.2. In Table 5.1 we only present estimates from surveys of post-election surveys to provide some comparison to the ANES.

[25] We note that the ANES estimates for Democratic vote share among Black voters are different from other data collections. ANES reports 86% of Black women supported the Democratic candidate in 2020. But the CMPS and news exit polls estimated a 95% Democratic vote share among Black women.

[26] There are consistent differences in the size of the gender gap by race prior to 2009. See Online Appendix Table A5.3.

Table 8 Proportion of vote for Democratic candidate by race and gender, 2008–2020

Election	White voters[1]			Black voters[1]			Latino voters[1]			Asian Am voters[2]		
	Women	Men	Gender gap	Women	Men	Gender gap	Women	Men	Gender gap	Women	Men	Gender gap
2008	45	39	6	99	100	–1	77	66	11			
2012	44	39	5	99	92	7	73	68	5	69	68	1
2016	41	37	4	93	84	9	74	67	7	79	69	10
2020	44	43	1	88	86	2	82	72	10	74	68	6

1. **Sources:** ANES Cumulative File 2008, 2012, 2016, and 2020

2. Post-election data are only available in 2012 National Asian American Survey; 2016 and 2020 CMPS

differences. Nevertheless, the data show that women of all races and ethnicities are more supportive of Democratic Party nominees for US president than men within their group across the last four elections.

These findings are consistent with the small, but growing, literature on the gender gap among minority voters. Political science research has identified a consistent gender gap in support for Democratic Party candidates among Black voters, though studies analyzing Asian American and Latino partisan candidate choice have been less conclusive. Some elections reveal a gender gap among Asian American or Latino voters, while others show only a small or insignificant difference between candidate preferences (Lien 1998; Garcia Bedolla, Lavareiga Monforti, and Pantoja 2007; Bejarano, Manzano, and Montoya 2011; Lizotte and Carey 2021).

Given the position of the two major political parties in the United States on gender and racial equality, it can be expected that we would find important variation both by race and by gender of the voter. But while both matter, the data here show that in terms of predicting partisan vote choice, there are greater differences by racial group than there are by gender.

The Significance of Race in Support for Democrats among Women Voters

In this section, we analyze the significance of race in vote choice for Democratic Party candidates among women voters in the United States between 1988, beginning around the time the gender gap was first noted, and through the most recent election of 2020, again utilizing data from ANES. In the previous section we presented the proportion of voters who supported Democratic Party candidates by race and gender. However, it remains a question whether or not race – and specifically being white – is a primary factor differentiating presidential vote choice among women voters. Not only does each election offer different candidates for voters to choose from, but every election also comes with a distinct electorate, the composition of voters changing with time and population replacement and also as a function of who decides to turn out to vote. Thus, variation in the quality of candidates for US president, their communications and mobilization strategies, and the reactions of voters all matter for the outcome of the elections.

In this analysis, we identify the key individual-level traits that predict Democratic vote choice in each election since 1988 using multivariate analysis. By comparing results across elections, we can ascertain whether or not the predictors of support for Democratic Party candidates vary by election, or if there are some traits that consistently predict partisan candidate choice across elections. If we find race to be a factor that consistently predicts vote choice, the evidence that the gender gap is driven by a race gap is more persuasive.

We specify statistical models that account for factors that prior scholarship has identified as being relevant to partisan candidate choice, including age, income, educational level, race, being from an immigrant family,[27] and religiosity[28] among the measures relevant to supporting Democratic Party candidates (Campbell et al. 1960).[29] The main difference between the model specified here and established practice is that we include respondent race as white as a dummy variable rather than the reference group. This model specification is consistent with traditional analyses of political behavior that have isolated particular groups into dummy variables in order to identify whether or not they differ from the reference group, which in this case is women of color. This strategy is distinct from the intersectional approach we took in earlier sections, and is deployed here to demonstrate that it is white women voters who are the outlier category among US women voters overall.

In addition to individual-level traits, and because we are predicting partisan candidate choice instead of turnout, the model is specified to include factors that account for whether or not the voter supports the Democratic nominee in that presidential election year. Therefore, we also include characteristics relevant to a voter's position in the economy (being employed and being a union member) that has been argued to play a role in vote choice. We include controls for the location of the voter such as living in the South[30] and urbanicity[31] given the long-standing geographic factors that influence partisan politics. Because the model is estimated for women voters only, past literature has indicated the importance of family status for women voters, and thus marital status is also included.

Using the aforementioned factors as independent variables in the model specification, we estimated nine logit models predicting voting for the Democratic Party candidate for each presidential election between 1988 and 2020 among women voters. The results from the logistic regression model estimations are detailed in Table 9. Because the equations estimated here are logit models, the data in the table show the log odds for those factors that reached statistical significance ($p<0.05$). Log odds allow us to present

---

[27] For immigration, the ANES cumulative file includes a question asking whether or not the respondent's parents are immigrants. ANES has not consistently collected data on the respondent's place of birth.

[28] Religiosity is measured as the frequency of attendance at religious services.

[29] See Online Appendix B for coding.

[30] South is defined using the Census Bureau's definition.

[31] Due to changes in confidentiality reporting, urban location of respondent is only available until 1996 in ANES publicly available files. For models for elections after 1996, urbanicity is excluded from the model.

Table 9 Predictors of voting for the Democratic candidate among women voters, 1988–2020, log odds

	Vote for Democratic Candidate (logit log odds)								
	1988	**1992**	**1996**	**2000**	**2004**	**2008**	**2012**	**2016**	**2020**
White	*.15*	*.29*	*.09*	*.23*	*.11*	*.07*	*.12*	*.11*	*.15*
Age		1.02	1.02	1.02					1.01
Education							1.13	1.35	1.33
Income				.74		.69	.83		
Immigrant family									
Never married		2.01					2.42	2.01	2.09
South				.50		.46	.70	.60	.67
Union member	1.67		4.12		3.17			1.59	
Employed									
Religious		.78	.72	.84	.83	.74	.73	.72	.73
Urban		1.70		–	–	–	–		
N	581	787	548	515	387	835	2085	1428	3146

Source: ANES Cumulative File

Note: Log odds derived from logistic regression using sampling weights; only those factors that are significant at p<0.05 are presented.

a standardized reporting for each independent variable in the model and allow us to understand the magnitude of the effect of that variable. To interpret log odds results, as the number rises above 1, it reflects a stronger positive relationship (and those that predict Democratic support). Numbers between 0 and 1 reflect a negative relationship (and those that predict Republican support) with numbers closer to 0 reflecting a strong negative relationship.[32]

Of those factors that reach statistical significance, most of the effects are consistent with expectations from the literature. In the models for the elections between 1992 and 2020, we find that those who attend church more regularly are more likely to be Republican. However, while the directionality of each factor is consistent with what we would expect, the other important finding we learn from the results of the models is that few variables consistently predict partisan vote choice over every election. Some factors play a stronger role in explaining partisan vote choice in some election years but not in others. This tells us that there are many features related to the specific characteristics of each election such as the types of candidates on the ballot and level of electoral competitiveness that influence which voters choose to turn out in any given election, and how those contours of the electorate affect the outcome.

Strikingly there is only one variable that reaches statistical significance for every election between 1988 and 2020, and it is whether the woman voter is white. In every election, white women are significantly less likely to vote Democratic compared to women of color, all other conditions held constant. The effect of race does not appear to be influenced by choices in statistical modeling since we find that even in model specifications that include other relevant variables such as partisan identification, race continues to have a constant and significant effect on partisan vote choice.[33] This analysis demonstrates that race is less subject to election-specific variation, and instead shows that being white is central to the formation of an individual's partisan candidate choice compared to other demographic factors. In terms of studying women voters, the implication is that race must first be factored into the analysis before we can estimate the role of gender. This conclusion is consistent with suggestions made by scholars who have studied women voters, including Huddy, Cassese, and Lizotte (2008), who argue that the partisan variation that occurs across subgroups of women is evidence that women cannot be framed as one coherent voting bloc but are rather characterized by political "disunity."

Taken together with the data demonstrating the systematic variation between white women and women of color in support for Democratic Party

---

[32] Online Appendix Table A5.4 presents full models.
[33] See Online Appendix Table A5.5.

candidates – with the former consistently voting majority Republican and the latter consistently voting strongly majority Democratic – it is clear that race is a crucial source of variation in how women voters express their preferences in presidential elections. That said, the data presented also demonstrate that gender remains important as well, and, in particular, that women of all races and ethnicities are more supportive of Democratic Party nominees compared to men.

Combined with the compositional over time data presented in the first section of this Element, the gender gap will continue to persist as long as women of color remain strong supporters of Democrats, and as African American, Latina, Asian American, and other women of color join the electorate. Compositional change in the American electorate has occurred over time as a function of enhanced voter enfranchisement of minority Americans along with the increase in immigrant populations as they naturalize to citizenship and bring their U.S.-born children into the polity. The future direction of women voters in terms of their partisan candidate preferences, however, is subject to change, and it is the political parties themselves that have the most to gain and alternatively the most to lose in a political context of dynamism, dealignment, and realignment. The implications of divergent patterns of partisan candidate support among women of color and white women voters in the United States, along with the companion set of results showing the gender gap is a race gap, are taken up next in the final section.

6 Race, Gender, and Dynamism in American Elections

Women are the most numerous and consequential voters in the American electorate, and while they lag in representation as elected officials at the national level, they are nevertheless the electorate that decides the winner. We began this Element by correcting three conclusions in the conventional wisdom on voting behavior, beginning with dispelling the notion that men dominate in elections. Men may be more prominent as candidates for office, but at the polling place, women have been the modal voter for more than half a century. In addition to being the largest gendered group in the electorate, women voters are diverse rather than monolithic. They vary in systematic and important ways, representing heterogeneous positions in partisan candidate choice that reside most significantly in race and ethnicity. The misleading stereotype that women support Democrats based on the consistent presence of the gender gap in voting has lured political analysts to disregard the fact that women of color are such strong supporters of Democratic Party candidates for US president that they carry white women with them, making the latter only appear to be Democratic by canceling out their persistent majority support of Republican Party nominees.

Taken together, these corrections to conventional understandings of women voters and the American electorate overall provide the opportunity to think differently about race, gender, and dynamism in elections. To do so, we introduced a new way of analyzing partisan candidate choice by conceptualizing the unequal constraints and opportunities for agency among voters that are based in their location at the intersection of gender and race hierarchies. Highlighting the compositional change in the population of voters due to immigration and voting rights legislation that expanded the electorate to include voters of color who were previously excluded identified an important source of dynamism in the American electorate.

Every election is a new electorate and is made so by generational replacement but also as a function of precisely this type of compositional change in the population. While change may be slow, it is ever-present, continuously transforming the electorate. Ignoring dynamism and continuing to rely on outdated concepts and assumptions – that men are the modal voter or that women across the board favor Democrats, for example – come with the price of blindness to both seeing relevant systematic variation among voters and being unable to anticipate and explain change in electoral politics in the United States.

The empirical evidence for our claims that the gender gap is a race gap, that being white is among the only consistent predictors of Republican party support among women voters, and that women of color are heavily Democratic because they have more constrained agency of choice, are based in large-N survey data collected across the last seven decades. It would be a mistake to interpret these data in isolation from dynamism in the political context that, during the same time period, witnessed the rapid racial and ethnic diversification of the US population to more than a third of Americans being non-white, accompanied by the reduction of formal barriers to enfranchisement for people of color.

Instead, our intersectional approach accounts for the legacy of disenfranchisement against women and people of color, the divergence between the modern Republican and Democratic parties, and the complicity of groups of Americans to keep the interlocking systems of oppression based in gender and race intact. In other words, our interpretation of the reasons why such distinct patterns in partisan candidate choice between white women voters and women of color voters are observed is because of their distinct intersectional positions of privilege, all of which is conditioned on historical context and the position of American institutions, among which political parties play an important role.

White women are still constrained by their gender, but they are privileged in having two actual choices in political party nominees. In contrast, women of color are relatively marginalized by both their gender and their race. As such, a much smaller proportion of women of color voters support Republican Party candidates compared to white women because of the anti-egalitarian policies of this party and its nominees run counter to the interests of women of color. Every woman voter may have the same Democratic and Republican Party candidate choices for US president on her ballot, but the equal viability of those options is a constraint in agency based in race and ethnicity.

Thus, the long-standing notion in political behavior research that individuals have equal agency of choice and of action is a problematic starting point, and one analysts must question rather than assume. It is this unsupported assumption that has blinded analysts from seeing and therefore accounting for the essential reality that individuals in the US polity are not equal. As demonstrated in the variation in partisan candidate choice among white women versus women of color voters, agency is constrained for the latter due to their marginalized intersectional position. This misunderstanding of assuming equal agency is why political analysts get it wrong when they portray women voters as a whole to be strong supporters of the Democratic Party. To better approach and understand voting behavior in a racially diverse electorate where women are the modal voter, aggregation may homogenize and cancel out the most important patterns that underscore the dynamism in American voting behavior.

Taken together, the empirical evidence detailed in the preceding sections and the interpretation of the analysis based on the intersectional conceptualization of agency and constraint generate three implications for the future of American elections: (1) compositional change of the electorate helps drive the formation of political party coalitions; (2) partisan dealignment and realignment are occurring and 3) identity politics will persist as an important feature of US electoral politics.

Compositional Change Informs Partisan Formation and Coalitions

Compositional change in the population as the result of immigration and increased racial diversity has generated anxiety among those who comprise the majority of the American population (Perez et al. 2023). Policy on immigration in the United States has most often been interpreted through a racial and ethnic lens, a pattern dating from the British colonial period, though who was defined as an outsider in these terms has changed over time. Xenophobic sentiment from negative tropes leveled against German newcomers (Franklin 1755), to Asian exclusion and the federal laws that followed mirrored in important ways the dynamics of the racialization of the Irish, Italians, southern Europeans, Jews, Slavs, and others as "less than white" that culminated in the 1924 National Origins Act (Ignatiev 1996; Jacobson 1999). More recently, policy barring immigrants from Latin America and predominantly Muslim nations is a stark reminder that the perceived desirability of newcomers remains an important modifier of a conditional welcome in US immigration politics.

In the contemporary context, compositional change has increased the racial and ethnic diversity of the population and, in so doing, incentivized political parties and elected officials to make immigration and race politics a political issue. While immigration policy has become a divisive partisan issue in recent decades, there have been periods of time when the parties were not in conflict with one another and where both of the two major political parties advocated for restriction (Gyory 1998; Tichenor 2002). Similarly, the 1965 passage of the landmark immigration legislation, the Immigration and Nationality Act, was supported by a large bipartisan majority, for few expected this law to have the effect it did on racial diversity (Masuoka and Junn 2013). In the two decades that followed, the positions of the Republican and Democratic parties on immigration policy have evolved from what Daniel Tichenor has described as one of "strange bedfellows" – where it was Republican President Ronald Reagan who signed a law that provided a path to citizenship for previously unauthorized immigrants and where it was Democratic President Bill Clinton who a decade later signed a punitive law that criminalized unauthorized immigration – into a politics of clear "dividing lines" between Republicans and Democrats.[34] Republicans are now seen as staunch restrictionists whose nominees for US president have pursued policies to "build a wall" and separate migrant children from their parents at the southern border, while Democratic Party presidential candidates are relatively progressive in their immigration policy positions, indicating a more welcoming stance for newcomers who are disproportionately non-white minorities in the United States.

Thus, immigration and, by extension, the politics of race and ethnicity have become politicized issues, with the two major political parties at opposing ends of a continuum representing restrictionist to more progressive positions. Parties and elites drive this policy development together with their voters, and on an issue as politicized and framed by racial and ethnic tropes as is the politics of immigration, the distinction between the Republican Party and the Democratic Party presents a stark choice for voters for whom immigration is an important issue and importantly for those whose are classified by race and ethnicity as something other than white. Thus, as the parties have moved toward opposite ends of the immigration policy continuum, voters who are less constrained by their race and ethnicity can choose on the basis of which party they agree with

---

[34] We refer to the 1986 Immigration Control and Reform Act and the 1996 Illegal Immigration Reform and Immigration Responsibility Act.

more and then sort accordingly. This degree of agency, however, is constrained for voters who themselves and their families may be the target of restrictionist immigration policy. In this way, compositional change informs how individual voters develop attachments to a political party, and partisan candidate choice for president is guided not only by ideological beliefs about the role of government or positions on economic policy issues, for example, but also by how one is affected by compositional change.

Compositional change in the population in terms of race and ethnicity is thus a source of dynamism in elections precisely because it informs not only the positions political parties take on immigration policy but also the contours of coalitions among voters. The full extent to which American voters are influenced by this population change and the immigration policy stances of parties in their partisan formation and loyalty to a political party remains to be seen, particularly for the most recent newcomers in the American electorate. But as the data on strong support for Democratic Party candidates among Latina and Asian American women – two groups with the highest proportion of immigrant and second-generation voters – attest, persistent Republican Party restrictionist positions on immigration and policies favoring criminalization and incarceration of migrants present an unwelcoming position and a constraint for minority voters to support Republican Party candidates.

Partisan Dealignment and Realignment Are Happening Now

The Republican Party and the Democratic Party are visibly divergent on policies related to the maintenance or attenuation of hierarchies based in both race and gender. Immigration policies are one prominent area of variation, as are the politics of reproductive rights. In contrast, the Democratic Party has marketed itself and pursued policies supporting gender equity, racial justice, and relatively progressive positions on sexual orientation and gender identity, while Republican Party policy at the national level has become dominated by candidates and platforms that have instead doubled-down on maintaining hierarchies and supporting "racially conservative" and "socially conservative" policy. While the internal dynamics of political parties are beyond the scope of this Element, the symbiotic relationship between parties and voters is evident in the data we presented on partisan candidate choice among women voters.

The extent of the polarization between the two major political parties and within American voters has been identified as a source of concern for the health of democratic politics. The fact that the electorate is dynamic due to immigration, compositional change as well as generational replacement, and that voters are open to conversion, are constants. There are periods when the ideological positions of the parties are changing in order to attract certain blocs of voters into their coalition and we argue is the present condition in US politics. This is an indicator of how parties are responding to what is happening in the electorate. While most of the attention among analysts has focused on political polarization, an equally important dynamic is the persistent dealignment of voters away from both parties and the accompanying rise in the proportion of American voters who call themselves independent of either party. This is the elephant in the room, and as evident as dealignment has been, it can only be ignored because elections are still, for the most part, contests between candidates nominated by the two major parties that voters must choose from. In tight elections, however, third parties can make a difference, but, more importantly, mobilizing independent and swing voters is key to winning.

Our analysis of the partisan candidate choice of women voters provides a window into the extent to which the positions taken by the parties on race and gender are increasingly leading to a systematic sorting of voters. The data presented earlier in this Element showed that the makeup of the Democratic and Republican parties is becoming more distinct over time. with the Democratic Party attracting greater race-gender diversity while the Republican Party remains comprised of white voters. The fractures in the political party system that are evident in the splintering of the Republican Party before and after the election of Donald Trump in 2016 and now into the present are an important indicator of partisan dealignment and realignment. Given the modal voter status of women in the electorate combined with the growth of the population of minority voters, the gender and racial composition of politicians will also change accordingly, though we might expect the path to elected office will remain more difficult for women overall and for Republican women (Holman, Merolla, and Zeichmeister 2022).

To understand the partisan dealignment and realignment that is occurring now, analysts will need to go beyond traditional New Deal realignment explanations based on voter conversion, mobilization, and generational replacement models, and instead incorporate additional explanations. In the present political moment, the population itself is changing due to immigration, and if not fully parallel to the creation of a Democratic majority in 1928–1936, that period and its dynamic is an important starting point for analysis (Andersen 1979). The significance of race and ethnicity in the modern context should also overlay the analysis (Schickler 2016). Embracing dynamic and intersectional approaches to analysis will contribute to a better understanding of the dynamics of voter dealignment from the two major US political parties, and help to chart the path of a new partisan realignment in the future.

Identity Politics Will Continue to Be Relevant

Identity politics has been derided most frequently by conservatives and members of the Republican Party when referring to equality and rights-based claims by women and people of color in particular. Responses to political movements such as Black Lives Matter, #MeToo, and the 2017 Women's March have denied the importance of identity categories in politics, while simultaneously reinforcing the race and gender hierarchies that make those categories politically relevant. Agency and constraint continue to be in tension, and among the most important imperatives of an "identity" politics is to assert power from a marginalized position whether based in a racial or ethnic category, or a broader minority identity as "people of color" (Perez 2021; Perez, Vicuna, and Ramos 2023).

When Barack Obama ran as the Democratic Party nominee for US president in 2008 he was often described as the Black candidate for president. When Hillary Clinton ran at the top of the Democratic Party ticket in 2016 she was described as the women candidate for president. But in those two elections, it was not necessary for John McCain to be described as a candidate with a racial modifier, nor was it necessary for Donald Trump to be labeled a white male presidential candidate, because they represented the default categories of race and gender in American political leadership. Nevertheless, and in an environment of deep political polarization and in the presence of a politics of grievance – some whose roots can be traced to the rapid racial and ethnic diversification of the population and the rise of women in politics – a variety of new angles of "identity politics" have emerged.

White Republican voters in particular have voiced their own version of identity politics, highlighting their aggrieved status perceived to be on the receiving end of political correctness and critical race studies, for example. White racial identity is the default racial category in American politics to the point where it is a status that until recently did not need to be named. The impact of strong identification with being a white American has been shown to have important effects on partisan candidate choice and voter mobilization (Weller and Junn 2018; Jardina 2019). A companion set of claims for upholding the virtues of traditional masculinity is among the newest set of claims in identity politics, with US Senators and other politicians from the Republican Party heralding the need for prioritizing manhood. Thus, identity politics is no longer the purview of traditionally marginalized groups of Americans, and now includes an updated set of categories vying for recognition.

Identity politics – whether rooted in a long history of discriminatory treatment based in gender and race or activated by a sense of grievance at what has been perceived to be lost – are the result of compositional change, policy innovation, and macro-structural conditions within and outside of US politics. Groups of Americans who have long been at the forefront of progressive politics advocating for social justice and policy change aimed at enhancing civil rights, voting rights, LGBT+ rights, and women's rights remain at the heart of identity politics precisely because patriarchy and racial hierarchy remain in place. All the same, the emergence of groups of voters representing new identities is very much a part of the dynamism in American politics we should expect, and these updated contours of identity politics will continue to be relevant to electoral politics and partisan candidate choice. Throughout these dynamisms, the significance of women voters in US elections remains constant.

References

Abrajano, Marisa, and Zoltan L. Hajnal. 2015. *White Backlash: Immigration, Race, and American Politics* (Princeton, NJ: Princeton University Press).

Acharya, Avidit, Matthew Blackwell, and Maya Sen. 2018. *Deep Roots: How Slavery Still Shapes Southern Politics* (Princeton, NJ: Princeton University Press).

Andersen, Kristi. 1979. *The Creation of a Democratic Majority 1928–1936* (Chicago, IL: University of Chicago Press).

Anzaldua, Gloria. 2022. *Borderlands / La Frontera: The New Mestiza*, 5th ed. (San Francisco, CA: Aunt Lute Press).

Bao, Xiaolan. 2006. *Holding Up More than Half the Sky': A History of Women Garment Workers in New York's Chinatown, 1948–1991* (Champagne, IL: University of Illinois Press).

Barkley Brown, Elsa. 1997. "To Catch the Vision of Freedom: Reconstructing Southern Black Women's Political History, 1865–1880," in *African American Women and the Vote 1837–1965*, ed., Ann D. Gordon, Bettye Collier-Thomas, John Bracey, Arlene Voski Avakian, and Joyce Avrech Berkman (Amherst, MA: University of Massachusetts Press), pp. 66–99.

Bauer, Nichole M. 2017. "The Effects of Counter-Stereotypic Gender Strategies on Candidate Evaluations," *Political Psychology*, 38(2): 279–295.

Bay, Mia E., Farah J. Griffin, Martha S. Jones, and Barbara D. Savage. 2015. *Toward an Intellectual History of Black Women* (Raleigh, NC: University of North Carolina Press).

Bejarano, Christina E. 2015. *The Latino Gender Gap in U.S. Politics* (New York: Routledge).

Bejarano, Christina E., Sylvia Manzano, and Celeste Montoya. 2011. "Tracking the Latino Gender Gap: Gender Attitudes across Sex, Borders, and Generations," *Politics & Gender*, 7(4): 521–549.

Bejarano, Christina E. 2014. "Latino Gender and Generation Gaps in Political Ideology." *Politics & Gender*, 10(1): 62–88.

Beltrán, Cristina. 2010. *The Trouble with Unity: Latino Politics and the Creation of Identity*. New York: Oxford University Press.

Blain, Keisha N. 2021. *Until I Am Free: Fannie Lou Hamer's Enduring Message to America* (Boston, MA: Beacon Press).

Blee, Kathleen M. 2002. *Inside Organized Racism: Women in the Hate Movement* (Berkeley, CA: University of California Press).

Blinder, Scott, and Meredith Rolfe. 2018. "Rethinking Compassion: Toward a Political Account of the Partisan Gender Gap in the United States," *Political Psychology*, 39(4): 889–906.

Bowler, Shaun, and Gary Segura. 2011. *The Future Is Ours* (Washington, DC: CQ Press).

Box-Steffensmeier, Janet, Suzanne DeBoef, and Tse-Min Lin. 2004. "The Dynamics of the Partisan Gender Gap," *American Political Science Review*, 98: 515–528.

Brown, Elsa Barkley. 1997. "To Catch the Vision of Freedom: Reconstructing Southern Black Women's Political History, 1865–1880," in *African American Women and the Vote, 1837–1960*, eds., Ann Gordon, Bettye Collier-Thomas, John H. Bracey, Arlene Avakian, and Joyce Berkman (Amherst, MA: University of Massachusetts Press), pp. 66–99.

Brown, Nadia E. 2014. "Political Participation of Women of Color: An Intersectional Analysis," *Journal of Women, Politics & Policy*, 35(4): 325–348.

Campbell, Angus, Philip Converse, Warren Miller, and Donald Stokes. 1960. *The American Voter* (Chicago, IL: University of Chicago Press).

Carey, Tony E., and Mary-Kate Lizotte. 2023. "The Ties that Bind: Public Opinion and Linked Fate among Women of Color," *Journal of Women, Politics & Public Policy*, 44(1): 5–19.

Carmines, Edward G., and James A. Stimson. 1989. *Issue Evolution: Race and the Transformation of American Politics* (New York: Cambridge University Press).

Center for American Women and Politics (CAWP). 2017. *Finding Gender in Election 2016: Lessons from Presidential Gender Watch* (New Brunswick, NJ: Barbara Lee Family Foundation).

Center for American Women and Politics (CAWP). 2022. "Gender Differences in Voter Turnout." New Brunswick, NJ: Center for American Women and Politics, Eagleton Institute of Politics, Rutgers University-New Brunswick. [https://cawp.rutgers.edu/facts/voters/gender-differences-voter-turnout] (Accessed September 2, 2022).

Chaney, Carole Kennedy, R. Michael Alvarez, and Jonathan Nagler. 1998. "Explaining the Gender Gap in US Presidential Elections, 1980–1992." *Political Research Quarterly*, 51(2): 311–339.

Chavez, Leo. 2013. *The Latino Threat: Constructing Immigrants, Citizens and the Nation*, 2nd Ed. (Palo Alto, CA: Stanford University Press).

Choy, Catherine Ceniza. 2005. "Towards Trans-Pacific Social Justice: Women and Protest in Filipino American History," *Journal of Asian American Studies*, 8(3): 293–307.

Collins, Patricia Hill. 2008. *Black Feminist Thought: Knowledge, Consciousness, and the Politics of Empowerment* (New York: Routledge).

Combahee River Collective Statement. 1977. [www.blackpast.org/african-american-history/combahee-river-collective-statement-1977/].

Conover, Pamela Johnston. 1998. "Feminists and the Gender Gap," *The Journal of Politics*, 50(4): 985–1010.

Cook, Elizabeth Adell, and Clyde Wilcox. 1991. "Feminism and the Gender Gap – a Second Look," *The Journal of Politics*, 53(4): 1111–1122.

Cook, Elizabeth Adell, Ted G. Jelen, and Clyde Wilcox. 1993. "State Political Cultures and Public Opinion about Abortion," *Public Opinion Quarterly*, 46(4): 771–781.

Corder, J. Kevin, and Christina Wolbrecht. 2016. *Counting Women's Ballots: Female Voters from Suffrage through the New Deal* (New York: Cambridge University Press).

Crenshaw, Kimberle. 2017. *On Intersectionality: Essential Writings* (New York: New Press).

Critchlow, Donald T. 2008. *Phyllis Schlafly and Grassroots Conservatism: A Woman's Crusade* (Princeton, NJ: Princeton University Press).

Darby, Seyward. 2020. *Sisters in Hate: American Women on the Front Lines of White Nationalism* (New York, NY: Little Brown).

Davis, Angela. 1981. *Women Race & Class* (New York: Knopf).

Dawson, Michael C. 1994. *Behind the Mule: Race and Class in African-American Politics* (Princeton, NJ: Princeton University Press).

de Beauvoir, Simone. 2011. *The Second Sex* (New York: Vintage).

Deckman, Melissa, and Erin Cassese. 2021. "Gendered Nationalism and the 2016 U.S. Presidential Election: How Party, Class, and Beliefs about Masculinity Shape Voting Behavior," *Politics & Gender*, 17(2): 277–300.

Dhingra, Pawan. 2007. *Managing Multicultural Lives: Asian American Professionals and the Challenge of Multiple Identities* (Palo Alto, CA: Stanford University Press).

Dittmar, Kelly. 2017. *Finding Gender in Election 2016: Lessons from Presidential Gender Watch* (New Brunswick, NJ: Barbara Lee Family Foundation & CAWP, Rutgers University).

Dudden, Faye E. 2011. *Fighting Chance: The Struggle over Woman Suffrage and Black Suffrage in Reconstruction America* (New York: Oxford University Press).

Espiritu, Yen Le. 1993. *Asian American Panethnicity: Bridging Institutions and Identities* (Philadelphia: Temple University Press).

Farris, Emily M., and Mirya R. Holman. 2014. "Social Capital and Solving the Puzzle of Black Women's Political Participation," *Politics, Groups, and Identities*, 2(3): 331–349.

Fox, Richard L., and Susan J. Carroll. 2013. *Gender and Elections: Shaping the Future of American Politics*, 3rd Ed. (New York: Cambridge University Press).

Fraga, Luis R., John A. Garcia, Rodney E. Hero, et al. 2011. *Latinos in the New Millennium: An Almanac of Opinion, Behavior, and Policy Preferences* (New York: Cambridge University Press).

Franklin, Benjamin. 1755. "Observations Concerning the Increasing of Mankind, 1951." Founders Online, National Archives. https://founders.arch ives.gov/documents/Franklin/01-04-02-0080.

Frasure-Yokley, Lorrie. 2018. "Choosing the Velvet Glove: Women Voters, Ambivalent Sexism, and Vote Choice," *Journal of Race, Ethnicity and Politics*, 3(1): 3–25 N-N.

Frasure, Lorrie, Janelle Wong, Matt Barreto, and Edward Vargas. 2016. The 2016 Collaborative Multiracial Post-election Survey (CMPS). Los Angeles, CA. https://doi.org/10.3886/ICPSR38040.v2.

Frasure, Lorrie, Janelle Wong, Matt Barreto and Edward Vargas. 2020. The 2020 Collaborative Multiracial Post-election Survey (CMPS). Los Angeles, CA.

Frymer, Paul. 1999. *Uneasy Alliances: Race and Party Competition in America* (Princeton, NJ: Princeton University Press).

Fujino, Diane. 2002. *Heartbeat of Struggle: The Revolutionary Life of Yuri Kochiyama* (Minneapolis, MN: University of Minnesota Press).

Fujiwara, Lynn, and Shireen Roshanravan. 2018. *Asian American Feminisms and Women of Color Politics* (Seattle, WA: University of Washington Press).

Garcia Bedolla, Lisa, and Becki Scola. 2006. "Finding Intersection: Race, Class and Gender in the 2003 California Recall Election," *Politics & Gender*, 2(1): 5–27.

Garcia Bedolla, Lisa, Jessica Lavariega Montforti, and Adrian Pantoja. 2007. "A Second Look: The Latina/o Gender Gap," *Journal of Women, Politics & Policy*, 28(3 & 4): 147–171.

Gay, Claudine, and Katherine Tate. 1998. "Doubly Bound: The Impact of Gender and Race on the Politics of Black Women," *Political Psychology*, 19(1): 169–184.

Gillion, Daniel Q., Jonathan M. Ladd, and Marc Meredith. 2020. "Party Polarization, Ideological Sorting and the Emergence of the US Partisan Gender Gap," *British Journal of Political Science*, 50(4): 1217–1243.

Gilmore, Ruth Wilson. 2007. *Golden Gulag: Prisons, Surplus, Crisis, and Opposition in Globalizing California* (Berkeley, CA: University of California Press).

Gilmore, Glenda. 2019. *Gender and Jim Crow: Women and the Politics of White Supremacy in North Carolina, 1896–1920*, 2nd Ed. (Chapel Hill, NC: University of North Carolina Press).

Goodier, Susan. 2012. *No Votes for Women: The New York State Anti-Suffrage Movement* (Champaign, IL: University of Illinois Press).

Groffman, Bernard, Christian Collet, and Robert Griffith. 1998. "Analyzing the Turnout-Competition Link with Cross-Sectional Data," *Public Choice*, 95: 233–246.

Grose, Christian R., and Karen Brinson Bell. 2023. "Philanthropy and Election Operations," *Journal of Election Administration Research and Practice*, 2(1): 24–31.

Gyory, Andrew. 1998. *Closing the Gate: Race, Politics, and the Chinese Exclusion Act* (Raleigh, NC: University of North Carolina Press).

Hajnal, Zoltan, and Taeku Lee. 2011. *Why Americans Don't Join the Party: Race, Immigration, and the Failure (of Political Parties) to Engage the Electorate* (Princeton, NJ: Princeton University Press).

Hamer, Fannie Lou. 1964. Speech at the 1964 Democratic National Convention [www.americanyawp.com/reader/27-the-sixties/fannie-lou-hamer-testi mony-at-the-democratic-national-convention-1964/].

Hancock, Ange-Marie. 2004. *The Politics of Disgust: The Public Identity of the Welfare Queen* (New York: New York University Press).

Hancock, Ange-Marie. 2015. *Intersectionality: An Intellectual History* (New York: Oxford University Press).

Hardy-Fanta, Carol. 1993. *Latina Politics, Latino Politics: Gender, Culture, and Political Participation in Boston* (Philadelphia, PA: Temple University Press).

Hardy-Fanta, Carol, Pei-te Lien, Dianne Pinderhughes, and Christine Marie Sierra. 2016. *Contested Transformation: Race, Gender, and Political Leadership in 21st Century America* (New York: Cambridge University Press).

Harris, Fredrick C., Valeria Sinclair-Chapman, and Brian McKenzie. 2005. *Countervailing Forces in African-American Civic Activism, 1973–1994* (New York: Cambridge University Press).

Harris-Perry, Melissa V. 2013. *Sister Citizen: Shame, Stereotypes and Black Women in America* (New Haven, CT: Yale University Press).

Hayduk, Ron. 2006. *Democracy for All: Restoring Immigrant Voting Rights in the U.S.* (New York: Routledge).

Holman, Mirya R., Jennifer L. Merolla, and Elizabeth J. Zechmeister. 2022. "The Curious Case of Theresa May and the Public that Did Not Rally: Gendered Reactions to Terrorist Attacks Can Cause Slumps Not Bumps," *American Political Science Review*, 116(1): 249–264.

Hondagneu-Sotelo, Pierrette. 1994. *Gendered Transitions: Mexican Experiencces of Immigration* (Berkeley, CA: University of California Press).

Howell, Susan E., and Christine L. Day. 2000. "Complexities of the Gender Gap," *Journal of Politics*, 62(3): 858–874.

Huddy, Leonie, and Nadya S. Terkildsen. 1993. "Gender Stereotypes and the Perception of Male and Female Candidates," *American Journal of Political Science*, 37(1): 119–147.

Huddy, Leonie, Erin Cassese, and Mary-Kate Lizotte. 2008. "Sources of Political Unity and Disunity among Women: Placing the Gender Gap in Perspective," in *Voting the Gender Gap*, ed., Lois Duke Whitaker (Urbana, IL: University of Illinois Press), pp. 141–169.

Hull, Akasha, and Patricia Bell-Scott, eds. 1993. *But Some of Us Are Brave* (New York: The Feminist Press at CUNY).

Iceland, John, and Rima Wilkes. 2006. "Does Socioeconomic Status Matter? Race, Class, and Residential Segregation," *Social problems*, 53(2): 248–273.

Ignatiev, Noel. 1996. *How the Irish Became White* (New York: Routledge).

Iversen, Torben, and Frances Rosenbluth. 2006. "The Political Economy of Gender: Explaining Cross-National Variation in the Gender Division of Labor and the Gender Voting Gap," *American Journal of Political Science*, 50(1): 1–19.

Jackman, Mary. 1996. *The Velvet Glove: Paternalism and Conflict in Gender, Class, and Race Relations* (Berkeley, CA: University of California Press).

Jacobs, Margaret D. 2014. *A Generation Removed: The Fostering and Adoption of Indigeneous Children in the Postwar World* (Lincoln, NE: University of Nebraska Press).

Jacobson, Matthew Frye. 1999. *Whiteness of a Different Color: European Immigrants and the Alchemy of Race* (Cambridge, MA: Harvard University Press).

Jaramillo, Patricia A. 2010. "Building a Theory, Measuring a Concept: Exploring Intersectionality and Latina Activism at the Individual Level," *Journal of Women, Politics & Policy*, 31(3): 193–216.

Jardina, Ashley. 2019. *White Identity Politics* (New York: Cambridge University Press).

Jordan-Zachery, Julia S. 2007. "Am I a Black Woman or a Woman Who Is Black? A Few Thoughts on the Meaning of Intersectionality," *Politics & Gender*, 3(2): 254–263.

Junn, Jane. 2017. "The Trump Majority: White Women and the Making of Female Voters," *Politics, Groups, and Identities*, 5(2): 343–352 .

Junn, Jane, and Natalie Masuoka. 2020. "The Gender Gap Is a Race Gap: Women Voters in U.S. Presidential Elections," *Perspectives on Politics*, 18(4): 1135–1145.

Kaufmann, Karen M. 2006. "The Gender Gap," *PS: Political Science & Politics*, 39(3): 447–453.

Kaufmann, Karen M., and John R. Petrocik. 1999. "The Changing Politics of American Men: Understanding the Sources of the Gender Gap," *American Journal of Political Science*, 43(3): 864–887.

Keyssar, Alexander. 2009. *The Right to Vote: The Contested History of Democracy in the United States, revised ed.* (New York: Basic Books).

Kim, Claire Jean. 1999. "The Racial Triangulation of Asian Americans," *Politics & Society*, 27(1): 105–138.

Klein, Ethel. 1984. *Gender Politics: From Consciousness to Mass* Politics (Cambridge, MA: Harvard University Press).

Koch, Jeffrey W. 2000. "Do Citizens Apply Gender Stereotypes to Infer Candidates' Ideological Orientations?" *The Journal of Politics*, 62(2): 414–429.

Larson, Kate Clifford. 2021. *Walk with Me: A Biography of Fannie Lou Hamer* (New York, NY: Oxford University Press).

Layman Geoffry. 2001. *The Great Divide: Religious and Cultural Conflict in American Party Politics* (New York: Columbia University Press).

Lemi, Danielle, Maneesh Arora, and Sara Sadhwani. 2022. "Black and Desi: Indian American Perceptions of Kamala Harris," *Journal of Women, Politics & Policy*, 43(3): 376–389.

Lett, Phoebe. 2016. "White Women Voted Trump. Now What?" *New York Times*, November 10, 2016 [www.nytimes.com/2016/11/10/opinion/white-women-voted-trump-now-what.html].

Leung, Vivien, Jae Yeon Kim, and Natalie Masuoka. Forthcoming. "Race in a Pandemic: Asian American Perceptions of Discrimination and Political Preferences in the 2020 Election," *Public Opinion Quarterly*.

Levendusky, Matthew. 2009. *The Partisan Sort: How Liberals Became Democrats and Conservatives Became Republicans* (Chicago, IL: University of Chicago Press).

Lewis, George. 2006. *Massive Resistance: The White Response to the Civil Rights Movement* (London: Hodder Education).

Lien, Pei-te. 1998. "Does the Gender Gap in Political Attitudes and Behavior Vary across Racial Groups?" *Political Research Quarterly*, 51(4): 869–894.

Lien, Pei-te, and Nicole Filler. 2022. *Contesting the Last Frontier* (New York: Oxford University Press).

Lien, Pei-te, M. Margaret Conway, and Janelle Wong. 2004. *The Politics of Asian Americans: Diversity and Community* (New York: Routledge).

Lizotte, Mary-Kate, and Tony Carey. 2021. "Minding the Black Gender Gap . . . ," *American Politics Research*, 49(5): 490–503.

Love, Nancy S. 2016. *Trendy Fascism: White Power Music and the Future of Democracy* (Albany, NY: SUNY Press).

Lowndes, Joseph E. 2008. *From the New Deal to the New Right: Race and the Southern Origins of Modern Conservatism* (New Haven, CT: Yale University Press).

Manne, Kate. 2017. *Down Girl: The Logic of Misogyny* (New York: Oxford University Press).

Mansbridge, Jane. 1986. *Why We Lost the ERA* (Chicago, IL: University of Chicago Press).

Manza, Jeff, and Clem Brooks. 1998. "The Gender Gap in US Presidential Elections: When? Why? Implications?" *American Journal of Sociology*, 103(5): 1235–1266.

Masuoka, Natalie and Jane Junn. 2013. *The Politics of Belonging: Race, Public Opinion and Immigration* (Chicago, IL: University of Chicago Press).

Masuoka, Natalie, Hahrie Han, Vivien Leung, and Bang Quan Zheng. 2018. "Understanding the Asian American Vote in the 2016 Election," *Journal of Race, Ethnicity, and Politics*, 3(1): 189–215.

Matos, Yalidy, Stacey Greene, and Kira Sanbonmatsu. 2021. "TRENDS: Do Women Seek 'Women of Color' for Public Office? Exploring Women's Support for Electing Women of Color." *Political Research Quarterly*, 74(2): 259–273.

Matos, Yalidy, Stacey Greene, and Kira Sanbomnatsu. 2023. "The Politics of 'Women of Color': A Group Identity Worth Investigating," *Politics, Groups, and Identities*, 11(3): 549–570.

McClain, Paula, Niambi M. Carter, and Michael C. Brady. 2005. "Gender and Black Presidential Politics: From Chisholm to Moseley Braun," *Journal of Women Politics & Policy*, 27(1–2): 51–68, https://doi.org/10.1300/J501v27n01_04.

McDermott, Monika L. 1997. "Voting Cues in Low-information Elections: Candidate Gender as a Social Information Variable in Contemporary United States Elections," *American Journal of Political Science*, 41(1): 270–283.

McGirr, Lisa. 2001. *Suburban Warriors: The Origins of the New American Right* (Princeton, NJ: Princeton University Press).

McRae, Elizabeth Gillespie. 2018. *Mothers of Massive Resistance: White Women and the Politics of White Supremacy* (New York: Oxford University Press).

Mendelberg, Tali. 2001. *The Race Card: Campaign Strategy, Implicit Messages, and the Norm of Equality* (Princeton, NJ: Princeton University Press).

Milbank, Dana. 2022. *The Destructionists: The Twenty-Five Year Crack-Up of the Republican Party* (New York, NY: Doubleday).

Milkman, Ruth, and Veronica Terriquez. 2012. "We Are the Ones Who Are Out in Front': Women's Leadership in the Immigrant Rights Movement," *Feminist Studies*, 38(3): 723–752.

Montoya, Celeste, and Mariana Galvez Seminario. 2020. "Guerreras y Puentes: The Theory and Praxis of Latina(x) Activism," *Politics Groups and Identities*, 10(2), 171–188.

Moraga, Cherrie, and Gloria Anzaldua. 2021. *This Bridge Called My Back: Writings by Radical Women of Color, Fortieth Anniversary Edition* (Albany, NY: State University of New York Press).

Morrison, Toni. 2021. YouTube [www.youtube.com/watch?v=ZGHsujbEvFI].

Murib, Zein. 2023. *Terms of Exclusion: Rightful Citizenship Claims and the Construction of LGBT Political Identity* (New York: Oxford University Press).

National Asian American Study, Asian Americans Advancing Justice and APIA Vote. 2013. "Behind the Numbers: Post Election Survey of Asian American and Pacific Islander Voters in 2012." www.naasurvey.com Press Release. April 5. http://naasurvey.com/2012-aapi-post-election-survey/.

Ngai, Mae. 1999. "The Architecture of Race in American Immigration Law: A Reexamination of the Immigration Act of 1924," *The Journal of American History*, 86(1): 351–376.

Ngai, Mae. 2005. *Impossible Subjects: Illegal Aliens and the Making of Modern America*. (Princeton, NJ: Princeton University Press).

Norrander, Barbara. 1997. "The Independence Gap and the Gender Gap," *Public Opinion Quarterly*, 61(3): 464–476.

Norrander, Barbara. 1999. "The Evolution of the Gender Gap," *Public Opinion Quarterly*, 63(4): 566–576.

Norrander, Barbara. 2008. "The History of the Gender Gap," in *Voting the Gender Gap*, ed., Lois Duke Whitaker (Champagne, IL: University of Illinois Press), pp. 9–32.

Och, Malinga, and Shauna L. Shames, Eds. 2018. *The Right Women: Republican Party Activists, Candidates, and Legislators* (New York: Praeger).

Ondercin, Heather L. 2017. "Who Is Responsible for the Gender Gap? The Dynamics of Men's and Women's Democratic Macropartisanship, 1950–2012," *Political Research Quarterly*, 70(4): 749–761.

Palmer, Barbara, and Dennis Simon. 2008. *Breaking the Political Glass Ceiling: Women and Congressional Elections*, 2nd ed. (New York: Routledge).

Pardo, Mary. 1998. *Mexican American Women Activists: Identity and Resistance in Two Los Angeles Communities* (Philadelphia, PA: Temple University Press).

Parker, Christopher S., and Matt A. Barreto. 2013. *Change They Can't Believe In: The Tea Party and Reactionary Politics in America* (Princeton, NJ: Princeton University Press).

Perez, Efren O. 2021. *Diversity's Child: People of Color and the Politics of Identity* (Chicago, IL: University of Chicago Press).

Perez, Efren O., Bianca Vicuna, and Alisson Ramos. 2023. "Taking Stock of Solidarity Between People of Color: A Mini Meta-Analysis of 5 Experiments," *American Political Science Review*, 1–7. https://doi.org/10.1017/S000305 5423001120.

Perez, Efren O., Jessica HyunJeong Lee, Ana Oxaca, et al. 2023. "Manifold Threats to White Identity and Their Political Effects on White Partisans," *Social Psychology and Personality Sci*ence. https://doi.org/10.1177/ 19485506231180650.

Phillips, Christian Dyogi. 2021. *Nowhere to Run: Race, Gender, and Immigration in American* Elections (Oxford University Press).

Philpot, Tasha. 2017. *Conservative but Not Republican: The Paradox of Party Identification and Ideology among African Ameri*cans (New York: Cambridge University Press).

Portes, Alejandro, and Robert L. Bach. 1985. *Latin Journey: Cuban and Mexican Immigrants in the United States* (Berkeley, CA: University of California Press).

Qian, Zhenchao, and Daniel Lichter. 2007. "Social Boundaries and Marital Assimilation: Interpreting Trends in Racial and Ethnic Intermarriage," *American Sociological Review*, 72(1): 8–94.

Ramírez, Ricardo. 2013. *Mobilizing Opportunities: The Evolving Latino Electorate and the Future of American Politics* (Charlottesville, VA: University of Virginia Press).

Ramirez, Mark. 2015. "Racial Discrimination, Fear of Crime, and Variability in Blacks' Preferences for Punitive and Preventative Anti-crime Policies," *Political Behavior*, 37: 419–439.

Reston, Maeve. 2016. "What Clinton's Loss Says About Women in Politics," *CNN*, November 9, 2016 [www.cnn.com/2016/11/09/politics/clinton-loss-women-politics/index.html]. accessed October 7, 2023.

Riismandel, Kyle. 2020. *Neighborhood of Fear: The Suburban Crisis in American culture, 1975–2001* (Baltimore, MD: Johns Hopkins University Press).

Rymph, Catherine E. 2006. *Republican Women: Feminism and Conservatism from Suffrage through the Rise of the New Right* (Chapel Hill, NC: University of North Carolina Press).

Sapiro, Virginia, and Pamela Conover. 1997. "The Variable Gender Basis of Electoral Politics: Gender and Context in the 1992 U.S. Election," *British Journal of Political Science*, 27: 497–523.

Schickler, Eric. 2016. *Racial Realignment: The Transformation of American Liberalism, 1932–1965* (Princeton, NJ: Princeton University Press).

Schlozman, Daniel, and Sam Rosenfeld. 2024. *The Hollow Parties: The Many Pasts and Disordered Present of American Political Parties* (Princeton, NJ: Princeton University Press).

Schmidt, Ronald Sr., 2021. *Interpreting Racial Politics in the United States* (New York: Routledge).

Schreiber, Ronnee. 2008. *Righting Feminism: Conservative Women in American Politics* (New York: Oxford University Press).

Segura, Gary, and Shaun Bowler. 2011. *The Future Is Ours: Minority Politics, Political Behavior, and the Multiracial Era of American Politics* (Washington, DC: CQ Press).

Seltzer, Richard A., Jody Newman, and Melissa Voorhees Leighton. 1997. *Sex as a Political Variable: Women as Candidates and Voters in US Elections* (Boulder, CO: Lynne Rienner).

Simien, Evelyn. 2006. *Black Feminist Voices in Politics* (Buffalo: State University Press of New York).

Sjoberg, Laura, and Jessica Peet. 2011. "A(nother) Dark Side of the Protection Racket: Targeting Women in War," *International Feminist Journal of Politics*, 13(2): 63–82.

Smooth, Wendy. 2006. "Intersectionality in Electoral Politics: A Mess Worth Making," *Politics & Gender*, 2(3): 400–414.

Sparrow, Bartholomew H. 2006. *The Insular Cases and the Emergence of American Empire* (Lawrence, KS: University of Kansas Press).

Stallion, Megan Thee. 2020. "Megan Thee Stallion: Why I Speak Up for Black Women," *New York Times*, October 13, 2020 [www.nytimes.com/2020/10/13/opinion/megan-thee-stallion-black-women.html].

Stout, Christopher T., Kelsy Kretschmer, and Leah Ruppanner. 2017. "Gender Linked Fate, Race/Ethnicity, and the Marriage Gap in American Politics," *Political Research Quarterly*, 70(3) (September): 508–522.

Strolovitch, Dara Z., Janelle Wong, and Andrew Proctor. 2017. "A Possessive Investment in White Heteropatriarchy? The 2016 Election and the Politics of Race, Gender, and Sexuality," *Politics, Groups, and Identities*, 5(2): 353–363.

Tanenhaus, Sam. 2013. "Original Sin: Why the GOP Is and Will Continue to Be the Party of White People," *The New Republic*, February 9.

Tate, Katherine. 1993. *From Protest to Politics: The New Black Voters in the American Electorate*. (Cambridge, MA: Harvard University Press).

Terborg-Penn, Rosalyn. 1998. *African American Women in the Struggle for the Vote, 1850–1920* (Bloomington, IN: Indiana University Press).

Thomsen, Danielle M. 2015. "Why So Few (Republican) Women? Explaining the Partisan Imbalance of Women in the U.S. Congress," *Legislative Studies Quarterly*, 40(2): 295–323.

Tichenor, Daniel J. 2002. *Dividing Lines: The Politics of Immigration Control in America* (Princeton, NJ: Princeton University Press).

Tien, Charles. 2017. "The Racial Gap in Voting among Women: White Women, Racial Resentment, and Support for Trump," *New Political Science*, 39(4), 651–669.

Verba, Sidney, Kay Lehman Schlozman, and Henry E. Brady. 1995. *Voice and Equality: Civic Voluntarism in American Politics* (Cambridge, MA: Harvard University Press).

Wallace, Sophia Jordán, and Chris Zepeda-Millán. 2020. "Do Latinos still support immigrant rights activism? Examining Latino attitudes a decade after the 2006 protest wave." *Journal of Ethnic and Migration Studies*, 46(4): 770–790.

Weglyn, Michi Nishura. 1966. *Years of Infamy: The Untold Story of America's Concentration Camps* (Seattle, WA: University of Washington Press).

Welch, Susan, and John Hibbing. 1992. "Financial Conditions, Gender, and Voting in American National Elections," *The Journal of Politics*, 54(1): 197–213.

Weller, Nicholas, and Jane Junn. 2018. "The Utility of White Racial Identity in Voting," *Perspectives on Politics*, 16(2), 436–448.

Whitaker, Lois Duke. 2008. *Voting the Gender Gap* (Champaign, IL: University of Illinois Press).

White, Ismail. 2007. "When Race Matters and When It Doesn't: Racial Group Differences in Response to Racial Cues," *American Political Science Review*, 101(2): 339–354.

White, Ismail K., and Chryl N. Laird. 2020. *Steadfast Democrats: How Social Forces Shape Political Behavior* (Princeton, NJ: Princeton University Press).

Williams, Linda Faye. 2003. *The Constraint of Race: Legacies of White Skin Privilege in America* (State College, PA: Pennsylvania State University Press).

Wolbrecht, Christina, and J. Kevin Corder. 2020. *A Century of Votes for Women: American Elections since Suffrage* (New York: Cambridge University Press).

Wong, Janelle. 2018. *Immigrants, Evangelicals and Politics in an Era of Demographic Change* (New York: Russell Sage Foundation).

Wong, Janelle S., S. Karthick Ramakrishnan, Taeku Lee, and Jane Junn. 2011. *Asian American Political Participation: Emerging Constituents and Their Political Identities* (New York, NY: Russell Sage Foundation).

Wu, Judy. 2022. *Fierce and Fearless: Patsy Takemoto Mink, First Woman of Color in Congress* (New York: New York University Press).

Young, Iris Marion. 1990. *Justice, Gender and the Politics of Inequality* (Princeton, NJ: Princeton University Press).

Zia, Helen. 2001. *Asian American Dreams: The Emergence of an American People* (New York: Farrar, Straus and Giroux).

Acknowledgments

We begin by expressing our gratitude to series editor Megan Ming Francis for her sage advice and patience in seeing this manuscript through to publication. We also benefited greatly from the incisive commentary and constructive suggestions of the reviewers. One question in particular prompted a full reorganization of the presentation of the sections in the Element. When originally submitted, the section on women of color was placed at the end, and one reviewer asked why we put women of color last? It became obvious that this was incorrect because it is in fact African American, Latina, and Asian American female voters who are consistent with the aggregate pattern of stronger support for Democratic Party candidates among women voters, while white women are the outlier in their persistent majority support for Republican candidates, including Trump in 2016 and 2020.

Identifying this positioning of white female voters first and women of color last revealed the powerful pull of the practice of treating whites and white men as the default categories in US politics. This is analogous to the definition of the "gender gap" in voting, where women's behavior is framed in comparison to men's, despite the fact that there are more women in the American electorate. Thus, the analysis of women of color now comes first, its placement consistent with our focus on dynamism in the composition of the American electorate and because the positionality of women of color as both gendered and racialized best exemplifies the concept of intersectionality.

We have benefited from the commentary and advice of many colleagues, as well as from presenting the work in progress at scholarly workshops and conferences at UC Riverside, UC Santa Barbara, Princeton University, Whittier College, Northeastern University, University of North Texas, University of Massachusetts Amherst, Cornell University, University of British Columbia, University of Notre Dame, and University of Missouri, the Asian American History group in addition to the Western Political Science Association, and the American Political Science Association annual meetings. We thank Chaerim Kim for her research assistance on the data analysis.

Jane acknowledges current and past USC colleagues: Jeb Barnes, Justin Berry, Christian Grose, Ariela Gross, Ange-Marie Hancock, Whitney Hua, Emily Liman, Gerry Munck, Carol Muske-Dukes, Christian Phillips, Ricardo Ramirez, Sara Sadhwani, Vanessa Schwartz, Jody Vallejo, Nick Weller, and Janelle Wong. In addition, thanks to colleagues in my other department of Gender and Sexuality Studies, including Karen Tongson, Eliz Sanasarian, and Atia Satar, who challenge me to think beyond disciplinary boundaries. Current USC PhD students have inspired me with their research and our shared interests: Tolu Babalola, Laura Brisbane, Raquel Centeno, Nancy Hernandez, Chaerim Kim, Jose Muzquiz, Karen Romero, Melissa Watanabe, and Kayla Wolf. Outside of my home institution, I have been enriched by the comradeship and insight of these colleagues, and I thank them for their generosity: Marisa Abrajano, Linda Alvarez, Nadia Brown, Niambi Carter, Kanchan Chandra, Kareem Crayton, Mai'a Cross, Leela Fernandes, Lorrie Frasure, Christina Greer, Meredith Horton, Kerry Johnson, Michael Jones-Correa, Claire Kim, Pei-Te Lien, Vlad Medenica, Jennifer Merolla, Chris Parker, Efren Perez, Reuel Rogers, Bat Sparrow, and Alvin Tillery. I thank my family, David, Eve, Juliet, and my mom, Sue Junn, for our shared values and their good cheer. While writing this book, I was inspired by two people who led by example and with immense courage. They are Cindy Gilbert and Sharyl Garza, Esq., two key players in supporting and winning compensation for women students at USC abused by a campus health center doctor. Sharyl and Cindy, I dedicate this book to you.

For Natalie, the formation of this Element spanned a number of major milestones including tenure, a move to a new institution and motherhood. Working on a manuscript on ideas that centered the unique intersection and the social and political constraints posed by race and gender during this period of time was probably no coincidence. It is clear now, looking back, that these professional and work experiences informed the underlining values and concepts we discuss in the Element. I feel privileged for the opportunity to work with colleagues in my new institutional home at UCLA. Building a program in race, ethnicity and politics with colleagues Lorrie Frasure, Matt Barreto, Efren Perez, Michael Chwe, Chris Zepeda-Millan, David Sears, and Gary Segura has been a deeply rewarding endeavor. I appreciate the welcoming spirit and inclusivity practiced by all of my colleagues in the UCLA Asian American Studies department. In particular, a thank you to Keith Camacho and Lucy Burns who provided invaluable support and a listening ear as vice chairs during my time as department chair. I thank those who have been great friends, colleagues, co-authors, mentors, research assistants, and/or writing buddies during the time of writing this Element and these relationships either directly or indirectly helped me think through many of the ideas presented in this Element. Thank you to Leisy Abrego, Edward Berdan, Nadia Brown, Niambi Carter, Nathan Chan, Orly Clerge, Christian Grose, Erik Hanson, Alisa Kessel, Jessica Lee, Greg Leslie, Vivien Leung, Joyce Nguy, Catherine Paden, Evangel Penumaka, Elizabeth Remick, Debbie Schildkraut, Ron and Rosemary Schmidt, MJ Strawbridge, Chris Stout, and Grace Talusan. I am thankful for the understanding I receive from my family Gordon and Olivia who are always forgiving when I ask for an "extra five minutes" to finish off what I am doing even though I typically need much longer. And a thank you to my extended family who have always shown their love and support. In writing this Element, I reflect on the bravery and resilience of the women in my family who serve as my foundation for understanding the uphill battles women of color have faced throughout American history and so dedicate this Element in memory of them. One particular childhood memory came to mind as we concluded writing this Element, which was the day my grandmother, Reiko, received her copy of the US government apology letter acknowledging its wrongdoing in the incarceration of Japanese Americans during World War II. She framed that letter and posted it next to the front of her door as a reminder to those who entered what had happened. Then as a child I had a sense of its importance but now as an adult the significance of that day and that act resonates deeply. Today I reflect on how I walked by that letter more times than I could possibly count and the impact that this had on me is probably immeasurable. From this, I learned from my grandmother how private acts like these are important and consequential expressions of our politics.

Cambridge Elements ≡

Race, Ethnicity, and Politics

Elements in the Series

A full series listing is available at: www.cambridge.org/EREP